MW01265546

YOUR MISTAKE IS NOT YOUR SIGNATURE

From Teacher to Prisoner to Principal

TERRANCE D. VICK

PublishAmerica
Baltimore

First printing

PublishAmerica has allowed this work to remain exactly as the author intended, verbatim, without editorial input.

ISBN: 978-1-61582-983-5
PUBLISHED BY PUBLISHAMERICA, LLLP
www.publishamerica.com
Baltimore

Printed in the United States of America

To Sonya Sueman

Never give up on your
dreams!

[signature]

ACKNOWLEDGEMENTS

I want to thank some people who extended to me the love and support I needed to complete this book. My son, Joseph, was not only the inspiration for the book but it is because of him that I continue to persevere. My wife, Christina, whose thoughtful suggestions and support were invaluable to my stability during this quest. She gave me the title for the book, 'Your Mistake Is Not Your Signature'. Dr. Tonya Huber, who ignited the spark in me by letting me know that only 5% of all people complete their books. Mrs. Sarbeth Farney, who was my mentor and editor for this book. Without you Mrs. Farney you and I know that this book would have never made it to print… Thank you! My appreciation to Mark Holland and the staff of J. Mark Holland and Associates for their legal advice and expertise. I, also, want to thank Calvin, Yolanda, Shawn, Meredyth, Danuyell, JeTaun and Mr. Kelly for their encouragement and confidence in me.

I began this book writing very critically about my father and all the things that I felt that he didn't provide for me as a child, only to realize as an adult how incredibly difficult it is to be a good father. I thank you Dad for everything that you gave to me, because what you did give to me was exactly what I needed to become the man and father that I have become today. I love you.

Finally, my mother, words cannot express how deeply I love you. You continue to believe in your baby boy and that I can achieve anything. Well...I did it!

TABLE OF CONTENTS

INTRODUCTION

Jesus said to her, "Did I not say to you that if you would believe you would see the glory of God?" Then they took away the stone from the place where the dead man was lying. And Jesus lifted up His eyes and said, "Father, I thank You that You have heard Me. "And I know that You always hear Me, but because of the people who are standing by I said this, that they may believe that You sent Me." Now when He said these things, He cried with a loud voice...

"Lazarus You Are Not Dead...Rise Up!"
John 11: 40-43

How did I get here? A dead situation, prison for me but for you it may be cheating on your spouse, selling drugs, lying about your taxes, stealing from the company, all dead situations that you said you wouldn't do again. **Lazarus you are not dead...rise up!** I promised myself and the All-Mighty over ten years ago that I would never return to prison. I know, I know, I know, I've made many promises in the past; some with good intentions, others so that I could feel good about myself. This one, to never return to prison, I swore on my life to uphold.

You see prison is not a place that one would wish upon anyone, not even your worst enemies. So, why then have I returned to prison? Back behind these same old walls that speak of death to all those that they encounter?

Is that you Lord speaking to me? If it is You Lord, give me a sign or something that I will know that it is Your voice that I hear. **Lazarus you are not dead...rise up**! I hear you Lord, and yes I will return to the prisons to tell those who are dead that You said in the name of the All-Mighty, "Rise up out of your dead situation and come forth." That if You can do it for me, a convicted felon, a liar, a cheater, an adulterous, a fornicator, who is also a Husband, a Father, a Teacher and making every effort to become a school administrator, a person who was after the heart of the All-Mighty, a person that needed not just a third but a fourth chance in life. That if You can raise up a Terrance Vick, then You most certainly can and want to raise up others from the dead who have been in similar situations.

This is my journey. One that started over ten years ago in the federal prison of Yankton, South Dakota. If I'm truly honest, I would say my journey dated backwards to my birth and early childhood. My pastor and spiritual father, Dr. Steve Houpe always reminds us that where you are in life is a direct manifestation of your thoughts. If you don't like where you are in life, then change how you think about yourself. So, it was over ten years ago that I decided that I wanted more out of life and that I wouldn't blame anyone for my shortcomings, not the judge, the jury, the attorney, or anyone else who thought negatively toward me. It was all on my shoulders...what I thought about myself and more importantly, what does the All-Mighty think about me?

"For I know the thoughts that I think toward you, says the Lord, thoughts of peace and not of evil, to give you a future and a hope. Then you will call upon Me and go and pray to Me, and I will listen to you. And you will seek Me and find Me, when you search for Me with all your heart. I will be found by you, says the Lord, and I will bring you back from your captivity." Jeremiah 29: 11-14

The poem Invictus reminds me,

"Out of the night that covers me black as a pit from pole to pole, I pray whatever gods may be for my unconquerable soul. In the felt clutch of circumstance, I have not winced nor cried outloud. Under the belonging of chance, my head is bloody but unbowed. Even beyond this place of wrath and tears, looms what horror of the shade but yet the minutes of the years find and shall find me unafraid. It matters not how straight the gate, how charged with punishment the scroll, I am the captain of my faith the master of my soul." Ernest Henley

If the All-Mighty thinks good thoughts about me and I believe that I'm in control of my own destiny then prosperity, health, joy, peace and happiness are within my grasp. I just needed to rise up out of my dead situations and come forth. The All-Mighty was calling me and I had to go. This may be my last chance and I didn't want to die in a dead situation. I didn't want to leave a legacy of "what if" or "what could have been." I didn't want others to speak over me like Martha spoke over Lazarus,

"Lord if only you had been here, my brother... Terrance Vick... would not have died."

ONE
Who Am I?

"Before I formed you in the womb I knew you; Before you were born I sanctified you; I ordained you a prophet to the nations" Jeremiah 1:5

I grew up like most people I suppose. We didn't have much but we didn't know it because no one in our neighborhood had much either. We were a family of ten. Seven siblings, I was at the end of the family line. I was the youngest boy of five, which wasn't any joy that I could recall. We had different fathers but we all had the same mother.

Forgive me if I don't call any of my siblings' half-brothers or half-sisters. When you come from the same mother and are raised in the same house, the only half is the half of chicken you get at the diner table. My father, who fathered the last three children, was there my entire childhood and teenage years. My other brothers and sisters even referred to my father as their father even though they did have contact with their own fathers, four others to be exact. Since mine was there, he bore the responsibility of attempting to raise all of us. Can't say my father did a good job of raising us but I give him credit for at least being there in presence. Maybe it takes a toll on any man to raise eight children, five to whom you were not the birth father. I come to a place of forgiveness of my father, for all the negative words that he spoke over me and my siblings, for all the times that I witnessed him beat my mother, for all the times I witnessed him drunk and belligerent, for all the times he allowed his mother, my grandmother, God rest her soul, to give my brother a Christmas and birthday gift right in front of me and my sister without giving either of us a gift, I forgive him! For he, my father, knew not what he did. I've come to realize that without forgiveness, those things that were done to you as an innocent child will haunt and torment you your entire adulthood. You will find yourself repeating the cycle of hatred to your children. Forgiveness is the most powerful force there is in the universe. This forgiveness takes time. I don't want to paint a false picture that I awakened one day and said, "I forgive you Daddy"; that's not how it happened. Once I was able to understand that I needed forgiveness, it was possible for me to forgive. "For by the measure that you forgive, forgiveness will be granted to you." A young child doesn't understand why negative words are spoken about him from the very person who is suppose to love him. He doesn't understand why his father, who is suppose to be his protector, allows anyone, even his mother to discriminate between his children. You don't understand why your father beats your mother or why he comes home from work complaining about the bills when he takes money every week to go gamble and drink. You don't understand these things as a child but you live through them. You keep going because to stop means death and everyone around you in the neighborhood is going through similar situations. Maybe this is just how things are suppose to be? Don't know but we don't talk about this stuff that goes on in the house, because what goes on in the house stays in the house. So you learn at a very young age to bury your hurts and frustrations deep inside and hope that they die with the memory of those negative things that have happened to you in your childhood.

Lazarus you are not dead…rise up! I hear you Lord, but I'm just a child and I'm not suppose to bear the burdens of adulthood. **Lazarus rise up…you are not dead.**

My mother, on the other hand, is my rock. She wasn't highly educated, she drank and swore constantly like a sailor but she loved her children. All eight of us were treated the same, although my older siblings will argue that she gave the younger siblings more. I never understood what more meant considering that more didn't keep our electricity from being shut off at times. More didn't keep my mother from humbling herself and going down to the welfare office to beg for food for her children to eat. More didn't keep my mother from going to charity lines asking for a donation for Christmas so that her children would have at least something to under the tree. These are things that I witnessed my mother do every day for her children. My mother made sure that her children always had something to eat and if there was only a little, she would refuse to eat. My mother always served my father first and children next. There were times when I wanted to give what little food I had to my mother but she would refuse to eat saying always that she wasn't hungry when I knew she hadn't eaten all day. My mother worked around the house all day and never missed a youth football or basketball game of mine. Her deeds said "I love you" even thought she rarely spoke the words. You know people by the work that they perform. If that saying is true, then my mother loved me with every inch of her being. Could someone please tell me why is it that urban children rarely hear a parent say "I love you?" Later as an adult, they seek the words "I love you" from all different sources like; relationships, jobs, careers, drugs and alcohol. Seeking love from unhealthy places and from hurting people only leads to dead situations and problems that take years to overcome and undo. Sometimes, you find yourself with people who say they love you only to take advantage of you. When you don't know what love looks like, or feels like what are you suppose to do?

Lazarus you are not dead...rise up!! But he/she said that they loved me. **Lazarus rise up...you are not dead.**

Academically, I was always in the top of my class but I attribute that to my competitive nature, because education wasn't stressed in our household. Don't get me wrong; my mother would come to the school if there were problems. However, we weren't forced to do our homework before we could go outside and play or to rise early in the morning to study, nor were we required to read books. Because of that I always struggled with reading. I never read until I went to go to school. In my reading group, I would determine when it would be my time to read. I would read ahead, so that I knew the words of the couple in the sentences that I would have to read. This was done so that no one would think that I was stupid or would laugh at me because I couldn't pronounce a particular word. Now because of my reading ahead, so as not to appear to be ignorant, I didn't comprehend what the other students who had read before me had read. So when an assignment was given over the reading, I would have to reread the entire assignment to be able to complete the assignment. It's amazing how many students do this, even to this day. I've come to believe that a child who has confidence, which is instilled in them through parents, isn't afraid to make mistakes; because he/she is confident, what others will think is not as important. My competitiveness drove me to want to be better than others who I perceived to have a better live style than I did. If I couldn't have better clothes or if I didn't live in a better house than they did, then academics would be the equalizer. I believe it is natural for children to be envious of others who they perceive to have a better life style than theirs. For this reason, I did pretty well academically and athletically. I recall as a youth telling myself that I wanted more in life than what I had seen around me. I didn't know necessarily how to achieve it, but I knew that there was something burning deep inside me that would not accept what I had seen others in my neighborhood accept. Everyone in my neighborhood was either in jail or working regular jobs that didn't provide enough financially for them to move out of section 8 housing. None of the older boys or girls went to college except two men who are still apart of my life to this day. How can you expect young people to become something that they haven't witnessed others who come from the same neighborhoods achieve? Maybe that's why we produce more drug-dealers than college bound students in our low income areas.

Lazarus you are not dead…rise up!! I hear you Lord, but everyone around me seems dead and college doesn't seem like a real option for someone like me, who comes from an impoverish low income neighborhood. "My grace is sufficient, even for those, Lazarus, who come from impoverish areas" **Lazarus rise up…you are not dead!**

I received an athletic scholarship to go play football in college when I graduated from high school.

Two
Continuing My Education

"For the people perish for lack of knowledge"

It was in college that I receive my first real education. Not education in the classroom sense but in life. It was in college that I learned how to take shortcuts, and at the time those shortcuts that I took appeared to be working. It would be in college that I acquired the "get over", or "get by" mentality. I found that if I went to class, took notes and never read the material I could still receive a B or C letter grade. That suited me just fine. When I really needed to focus, I could focus enough to pass any test that the professor would give. I was more concerned about the women in college. In high school, the women didn't seem interested in me at all even though I graduated in the top percent of my class and was a high school Blue-Chip All-American football player. So, I wanted to graduate from college with a degree in knowing how to attract women. Like the song from Waylon Jennings,

"I was looking for love in all the wrong places, looking for love in too many faces."

It's a very dangerous thing when you're young and you're trying to find your place in life while searching in the dark. You run into a dead end street and go places that lead to nowhere. Many mistakes could be avoided if only you had some light to be able to see where you are actually traveling. When you travel in the dark and your vision is blurry, the actual destination always takes longer, because you always have to stop to ask someone if you're going in the right direction. For those of us who don't stop to ask for direction because of our pride, we drive in circles wasting even more time and money. So, this was me, traveling in the dark with no direction and living a life of chance. Making mistakes and accepting that mistakes have to be made in order for me to make any progress. Deep inside, I was a scared little boy who yearned for his father to give him some guidance. I needed him to tell me that everything was going to be all right and to stay focused on the goal. I wanted that help badly, so badly that I could taste it. Because I didn't receive it, I found the next best thing…a woman. Now, I'm not implying that women are bad; that would be ludicrous to imply. What I am saying is that when you have a confused, frighten, scared young man with low self esteem, who is looking to be confirmed through love, it can only lead to trouble for any young woman who crosses his path. No woman should be the target of a man's insecurities and insults in order to build his self-esteem. Unfortunately, this burden is happens frequently to women, who date insecure men. If the woman isn't verbally abused, she usually becomes physically abused. Sometimes, verbal abuse takes more time to heal than the physical abuse. I regretfully acknowledge that I spent a great deal of my young adult life verbally not physically abusing women. Because I witnessed my father physically abusing my mother, I never forgave myself for not protecting her, even though I was only a child. Hurting people hurt people, and sick people need help. I was both hurting and sick inside with no where to turn.

I found myself for the first time experimenting with drugs and alcohol. I can't lie, the drug that I experimented with was marijuana. I wasn't big on weed like everyone else but I adopted the motto "when in Rome do as the Romans" and like I said, everyone was smoking it. Peer pressure can be a dangerous thing especially for someone who lacks self-esteem. Everyone wants to think of themselves as leaders, but true leaders are the people who face the masses and say "No" despite what others will think about them. I didn't know how to stand up because I never had.

Therefore, I went along to be accepted by others which meant that I had to sacrifice my principles. By the way, what were my principles? What did I stand for…I didn't know? My father had never shared with me our family values. I guess it was his fault, I blame him for everything else, I might as well blame him for not teaching me about principles…better to blame my father then to accept responsibility for myself.

It was during my first two years of college that I would experience my toughest challenge…I tore the ACL in my knee during a football game. I had never been injured while playing sports but this injury required me to do some real soul searching. You see, I was considered one of the best defensive backs to have come from Wichita, Kansas in years. However, when I went to college, I was competing with the best players from across the nation. I had the athleticism to compete but I lacked the necessary confidence. As a defensive back, if you lack confidence then you're finished. So, when I tore my ACL, my football career ended. I would never play major college football and I would have to return home to Wichita, Kansas as a failure and listen to people say to me, "Man, I thought you were going to make it, you were so talented." Without football, it seems my life is over. Don't want to be subjected to people thinking I'm a failure.

Lazarus you are not dead…rise up! God, so many people where counting on me to make it and I can't face them knowing that I failed. **Lazarus rise up…you are not dead.**

I received a full academic scholarship, "Grow Your Own Teacher", to Wichita State University.

Still needing to belong to something, I joined a fraternity at Wichita State University. Fraternity life is cool….I can become anyone that I desire to become, because when your frat, your frat. People don't really want to know who you are as a person but what you represent with your purple and gold colors. Fits me perfectly, because truth be told, I haven't really discovered who I am. By the way who am I? Never had anyone tell me who I am…I know that I can blame my father for this one. He was supposed to tell me who I am. I'm not responsible for figuring it out myself; this is clearly my father's responsibility. I guess I'm this guy who enjoys all this attention from women when I perform on stage during step-shows. Sounds like a winner to me, beside any attention is good attention, and I've been craving some attention for a long time. I like this person…I don't know who this person is but everyone else seems to like this person so maybe this is who I'm suppose to be.

My father seems to like the new me as well. I say this because for the first time that I can recall my father speaks highly of me. He says things like, "my son surely does have many beautiful women," "look at all the women that my son has," and my favorite "my son is a playa!"

So for all the accomplishments that I had received over the years academically and athletically, the only compliment I would receive from my father would come at the expense of women.

By this time I started taking my college courses a little more seriously. Once I started to settle into a good routine an incident occurred that would challenge how I felt about myself.

I recall setting in the classroom and the professor explaining to the class that a project was needed in order to complete the course. We were given a task which required students to work in groups. Although I was the only African-American in the class, everyone knew me. However, I was not ask to participate in any group.

Rejection, even at a higher learning institution! The professor waited to see if any group would invite me to join but no group did. To make matters worse, the professor had to announced to the class that I didn't have a group. He asked if any group would be willing to include me. None volunteered. Eventually he placed me in one of the groups; however, it was clear to me that they didn't want to work with me and this rebuff tore at the core of my being.

I was already dealing with rejection from my father. To have to face rejection in school was devastating to me. In my childhood, school was the one place where I found refuge. Now, even that sanctuary was starting to crumble. I remember trying to convince myself that everything would be ok! I would be the first teacher hired because of the need for male and African-American teachers. I would get the last laugh…but deep inside it wasn't funny; I was hurting and felt alone.

Why did this have to happen to me Lord? I'm one of the smartest people in this class. They were seeing me through the color of my skin rather than my ability to perform within the classroom. Actually they were not seeing me at all, it was as if I were transparent and they saw right through me.

Is this what Ralph Ellison meant when he wrote "Invisible Man?" I feel invisible right now…wish my father would tell me how to channel this frustration and loneliness that I'm feeling inside. It's his fault that I'm invisible. He should have put substance inside me so that others would recognize that I'm here, setting right next to them.

My real world education would come to an end. I would graduate from college knowing that the only thing that really mattered to me would be the women I conquer, and never allowing anyone to make me feel invisible again. Women matter to my father, so they matter to me. Besides, it feels good to hear my father say that he's proud of me. I crave to have my father's approval even if it means that I'm going to hurt people along the way. I will ask for forgiveness later…I need to have my father's approval!

Lazarus you are not dead…rise up! Lord please forgive me for all the pain I caused others. I never meant to hurt anyone, but it was the only way to get my father's approval. **Lazarus rise up…you are not dead.**

I graduated from Wichita State University with a degree in Elementary Education and accepted a job teaching second grade in the Wichita Public School District.

THREE
Robbing Peter to Pay Paul

I've finally found my passion...its teaching! My students are awesome and I receive 100% parental support. Life is good for me right now! I love my job, I have multiple women who are interested in me and I'm making more money than my parents ever made, and my principal, the only other African-American male in the building, is becoming more and more like the father-figure I so desperately have sought. Nothing could go wrong right now.

Spoke too fast! My principal, who has taken on the role of a mentor to me, seems to be acting indifferent toward me. Could it be the teacher who is rumored to be romantically involved with him constantly finds herself in my classroom helping me as a first year teacher? Don't get me wrong, I think she is an attractive woman but he is my mentor and somewhat like a father-figure to me. I would never get involved with this woman, it's not worth it! She just told me that she isn't involved with him...I guess that makes her fair game.

Why can't I go to the Million Man March? This is an historical event that African-American men will remember and tell their children for generations. He thinks that it will be a bad political move if I go. I don't care! He seems to be making excuses for me not to go but I bet you she has something to do with this decision. I'm not even fooling around with her.

Wait a minute…this looks all too familiar to me. I know…my father's behavior, that's what this looks like.

Why do men compete over territory when the land is plentiful? Thought I had a real mentor only to run into a father impostor.

He had an opportunity to really make a difference in my life. He could have helped me.

Once again, it's my father's fault…it has to be. Can't be mine, I didn't do anything. I promise I didn't sleep with that woman!

Made a decision…I will become my own man! Never going to look toward another man for guildance.

Wait…what is a man? My father is a man isn't he? Not the type of man I want to become. I want to be a better man, but I don't know how. I have never seen an example of what a better man looks like. Is it even possible to become a better man, when all the men I know seem to possess similar characteristics of my father? Maybe I am a man? I do pay my own bills and I don't ask anyone for anything. I do me; and doing me has gotten me this far. Not bad at all for someone with my background?

My neighbor is really cool…I really like this dude. I know, I know, I know…he sells drugs but he seems like a good brother and besides he's making paper! Can't knock him for that, he's doing what he has to do to make it.

He probably didn't have a father in his life to teach him the importance of hard work, so he probably had to find his own way. Yeah, I'm sure it's his father's fault…I was right… he didn't have a father growing up, so he had to do what he had to do.

I was lucky…I was good enough in football to get my college tuition paid. If it weren't for football, I don't think I would have gone to college. With the exception of my brother Calvin, who was one year older than I, my siblings didn't go to college. Track, was his ticket like football was mine. I guess I could have been in that same situation selling drugs if I hadn't gone to college.

Because I know one thing…I wasn't going to live the way my parents lived. Don't get me wrong, my parents did the best that they could do with the education that they had. I will be forever grateful that they did keep a roof over my head and I never went to bed hungry. I think they could have done more...especially my father. Despite only having a high school education, he really was a smart man but he spent too much of his life complaining instead of just making it happen. Besides... he had his opportunities, he just didn't take them. If I get an opportunity, I'm going to take it. I will not be like my father who missed living a more successful life.

What did you say Lord...there are not shortcuts to success!

I hear you but...I want what ever man wants...the American Dream, and besides that the men who are out there selling drugs...seems like they all have that dream. They are living large!

But who am I kidding...I'm a teacher and these kids really respect and admire me and I would never do anything to jeopardize their trust. They love me and need me, but I don't know what I would do if the opportunity presented itself. Probably wouldn't get caught anyway...seems like no one ever gets caught. If I did take that chance, rest assured, I'm smarter then any of those men.

I would probably be like Tony Montana in the movie "Scarface" running stuff...yea that's how I would do it.

I hear you Lord...good things come to those who wait!

But think of all the good I could do if I had just a little more...I could make sure all my students had winter coats, adequate shoes on their feet, I could do some good with some extra money. I would be like Robin Hood...taking the money I made from the people who get high and doing something good with it.

But who am I kidding...I'm a teacher and proud to be a teacher!!!

Let me get this right man...all I have to do is connect you with my neighbor? Since we are related you're going to owe me big time.

What do you mean...you don't want to meet him! He's coming all the way from Oklahoma because you said you would "hook him up."

Oh...I get it now. You want me to get the money from him and bring it to you and you will in return give me the drugs to take to him, because in your line of work you don't like to meet new people. I would be sort of like the "middle man" huh?

But I'm a teacher...I shouldn't be getting involved in this mess...I could get caught and I would be in big trouble.

Yea…but I'm like the "middle man!" That's not considered a drug dealer. I'm not even selling anything…I'm just transporting drugs from one person to the next. That's not selling drugs…it's transporting…big difference!

But I'm a teacher…yeah, but maybe this is my opportunity to make some extra money and do some good deeds with that money.

That was easy…and I made three thousand dollars without even doing anything, but it was a one time deal.

I'm a teacher and I'm never doing that again, or at least not the way I did it the last time. I could do it in a way that would provide less risk on my behalf.

What do you mean…you're coming in town again and you want me to get in contact with my neighbor!

Shouldn't do it…said it was a one time deal and I meant it…right! I did do some good with that money. I was able to buy winter coats for a few of my students, this time if I decide to do it, I could buy myself a few things that I always wanted.

What am I saying…I'm a teacher and I could get caught.

Yea I know…no one ever gets caught and besides I'm smarter then these guys. College was a breeze to me and I would bet my life they never went to college, so I'm smarter.

Money is flowing now and I'm starting to think maybe I shouldn't be teaching anymore. Teaching takes up too much of my time when I could be perfecting my skills as a "middle man"… I really could become the next "Scarface"

Who am I kidding…I'm a "middle man" I mean teacher or is it "middle man"

July 14, 1997…What do you mean…"put my hands behind my back, I didn't do anything!!"

What am I going to do now…how am I going to get out of this situation?

Lord if you're listening…I really need your help to free me from this jam. I can't go to jail…I'm a teacher and what would those children who believed in me think? You have to help me…I promise I won't do it again!

No response huh…where is the Lazarus you are not dead rise up…huh where is it…It's my father's fault. If only he had really been in my life to give me guidance, then he could have told me that I was going down the wrong path. Because he let me do my own thing the way I wanted to do it, I'm now in this messy situation…and I'm scared to death as to what is going to happen to me. I have to make my own decisions because I don't have anyone to help me…I'm on my own!

D.E.A. is offering me a deal… said that they are willing to release me back to the streets if I become an informant. They don't want me. They said they knew that I was only acting as a "middle man." They want my neighbor, the person from whom I purchased the drugs.

Sounds good to me…besides some one ratted on me to save themselves…why shouldn't I do the same!

D.E.A. is constantly changing their agreement with me…first, it was the guy out of town, from whom I received the drugs that they wanted …now, they want a million dollars of drug money off the streets.

Shoot…if I knew how to get a million dollars of drug money then I wouldn't be here in this situation. Something doesn't sound right…if I become an informant I'll never be free of them until I am found dead somewhere.

Not worth it…I made this bed now I have to lie in it, even though the bed seems to be on fire.

Lazarus you are not dead…rise up!

Your speaking to me now Lord…where were you when I needed you…I'm in serious trouble but I know what I must do, which is to accept my responsibility for the poor choices that I made…the money wasn't even worth it!

Lazarus rise up…you are not dead.

"Lazarus, have I not commanded you? Be strong and of good courage; do not be afraid, nor be dismayed, for the Lord your God is with you wherever you go." Joshua 1:9

I was released from the custody of the D.E.A. with no charges brought against me…so I thought. I was offered a new teaching position with a middle school. After I informed my new principal of what had transpired over the summer with the D.E.A. and assured him that I did not have any charges pending against me, he offered me the position with a ten thousand dollar increase in salary.

FOUR
You Reap What You Sow

"Do not be deceived, for whatever a man sows, that he will also reap"
–Galatians 6:7

Being released from the custody of the D.E.A. without any pending charges gives you a funny feeling. I didn't know what to expect; so I didn't know how to approach the situation or what to do. I retained an attorney, whose job was to inform me as to what was happening with my case. Retaining the attorney cost me two thousand dollars. He explained to me, after I shared with him what all had happened with the D.E.A., that there were no charges pending against me. He advised me not to speak with the D.E.A. without him being present and most importantly not to do anything that would give the D.E.A. any more evidence to build a case against me. I assured him that I could do those two things, and I walked away feeling quite confidant that I had dodged a major bullet. I didn't even mind that I had given him two thousand dollars, if it would save me from the embarrassment of going to jail.

The other concern I had was whether or not I should accept the new teaching position with the middle school. I had already shared with the principal that I had a problem over the summer but after speaking with my attorney, I had assured my principal that everything was okay.

Because of this, I accepted the job to teach middle school math and coach the boy's basketball team. This was the time in my life that Danuyell, would come and play a vital part in helping me through this tragic and troublesome time.

Everything was going good for me, until that dreaded day of March 18, 1998… A day that I will never forget! This was the day that I reaped all that I had sown and what I had sown was a heap of trouble for myself.

The way it happened is somewhat of a blur to me, but I do remember that I was dismissed from school early because I had completed parent teacher conferences and I was at my townhouse.

There was a knock at my door around 2:00 p.m. As I looked through the peep hole, I saw a police officer. The police officer informed me that he had a report that my car had been stolen and needed me to come to his police car and complete a stolen car report. I proceeded to put on my shoes and followed the police officer to his car. At the end of the building were ten D.E.A. officers waiting for me. The D.E.A. officers then asked me to place my hands behind my back. After handcuffing me, they returned me to my townhouse and ask if I possessed any guns or drugs. I informed the officers that I didn't possess any guns or drugs but they searched the house anyway. While several of the officers were searching the house for weapons and drugs, several other officers were reading me my rights. Then, they took me to the County jail and booked me.

This all happened March 18, 1998, eight months after the D.E.A. had released me from the original arrest. I had been employed for seven months at the middle school and now it had all come to an end.

That night while I sat in the jail, I watched the television and witnessed the news correspondent report live from the middle school that a teacher had been arrested earlier on drug charges. I remember thinking that not only was this reporting wrong but that my teaching career was finished. People believe what they see on the television and assume that when a story is reported, especially one of this magnitude, it must be accurate. I went into my cell and started crying…wondering why this had happened. What did I do to deserve this cruel fate? There would be no answer…just tears of frustration, embarrassment and fear of what was going to happen to me.

It would be during this tumultuous time that Danuyell would suggest to me that I keep a journal of how I was feeling. I'm not going to lie…it was difficult to write because all that was running through my head was how all of this would impact the students that I had taught the last few years. I couldn't get their faces out of my mind and I wondered constantly, what they thought about me? Did they lose trust in me? Did they even care?

I know, I know, I know…with everything that was happening; me on the television, me in the newspaper, and people making comments about me that I didn't even know, the last thing with which I should have been concerned is what other people thought about me. But what my students thought tormented me because they mattered and meant everything to me. You see, it was at this point that I realized how important teaching was to me, because I was in jeopardy of losing it.

They say you don't miss a good thing until it's gone…well teaching was that good thing to me, and she was long gone never to return! I never cried about any woman the way I cried about teaching…I truly loved her with all my heart.

Since I couldn't write about my feelings, I did the next best thing and wrote poetry for other inmates who couldn't express themselves in letters and wanted me to write poems on their behalf to their loved ones. This was funny to me since English was never my strong suit in school. Math was what I taught as a teacher but I have to admit that this writing poetry for others was therapeutic to my mind and soul. It allowed me to focus on others instead of my own problems…and the poems flowed so effortlessly on the paper, I really thought that maybe I missed my calling.

Although I was writing now, I still had to deal with my own battles. I had fired my first attorney and hired a new attorney that said that he would fight for me. While I was waiting to be sentenced, I was being transported from jail to jail since I was in the custody of the federal government. There was no place over the six months that I stayed confined for any length of time. As my sentencing was approaching, I found myself turning to God and reading His Word.

I know at this point what some of you will say…everyone in prison finds God, that's nothing but a jailhouse religion, and my favorite…why did you have to go to jail to find God? I don't know how to answer those questions but to say to you that if people in jail don't need God...then who? I believe God is always with us but sometimes it takes us a fall like the one I had for us to realize that we can't escape death unless something higher than ourselves rescues us. I say death because when you're in prison you feel like you're slowly dying. Prison eats at your soul and mind slowly, causing you to have many, many thoughts. Some thoughts are of killing yourself, because the burden has become too heavy for you to carry. You just want to die because ending it seems to be the easiest way to make it stop the tormenting.

I, too, had those thoughts...but for me it was God's Word that kept me going and assured me that this too would pass. I was facing a storm that appeared to be raging wildly out of control in my life and I needed a sign...anything that would assure me that God hadn't forgotten me. I would get the sign...but not in the way that I was asking!

I was due to appear for sentencing the next day...when something out of the ordinary happened to me that would forever change my prospective on life. As I mentioned earlier, I was not one who went to church regularly or could quote any scripture with the exception of John 3:16.

"For God so loved the world that He gave His only begotten Son, that whoever believes in Him should not perish but have everlasting life."

A scripture that everyone knows! I was just looking for something to get me out of this trouble into which I had fallen ... and to do it in a hurry. I had been locked up five months and I missed home and would have done anything to escape. Little did I know, I was going to have to steady the course?

Meanwhile in my reading, I came across the story of blind Bartimaeus. For those who aren't familiar with the story here it is...

"Now they came to Jericho. As He went out of Jericho with His disciple and a great multitude, blind Bartimaeus, the son of Timaeus, sat by the road begging. And when he heard that it was Jesus of Nazareth, he began to cry out and say, "Jesus, Son of David, have mercy on me!" Then many warned him to be quiet; but he cried out all the more, "Son of David, have mercy on me!" So Jesus stood still and commanded him to be called. Then they called the blind man, saying to him, "Be of good cheer. Rise, He is calling you." And throwing aside his garment, he rose and came to Jesus. So Jesus answered and said to him, "What do you want Me to do for you?" The blind man said to Him, "Rabboni, that I may receive my sight." Then Jesus said to him, "Go your way; your faith has made you well." And immediately he received his sight and followed Jesus on the road. Mark 10:46-52

I returned into my cell and cried, cried, cried out loud saying Jesus, Son of David please do not pass me by. The federal government is trying to convict me of things that I didn't do and I need you tomorrow when I enter that court room to be my attorney. I'm scared and frighten but I don't have anything to lose...I need you...please don't pass me by! I know that I don't know you the way I should but I'm going to call out your name, Jesus...until you come by here and answer my prayer.

This prayer continued for two hours until I cried myself to sleep...Jesus, Son of David please do not pass me by...

The next morning I appeared before the U.S. District Judge Belot, who had a reputation of being the harshest judge when it came to sentencing, and I cried when he asked if I understood the charges being brought against me before I accepted this plea agreement.

To my surprise U.S. District Judge Belot cursed the United States prosecuting attorney and my attorney, telling them both that it appeared to him that I was an intelligent man who apparently didn't agree with this plea agreement.

When both attorney attempted to object at the same time...U.S. District Judge Belot said, and I quote..."Get the Hell out of my courtroom and don't come back until your client understands what he is agreeing to!"

Lazarus you are not dead...rise up!

Thank you, thank you, thank you Jesus...if I only had known you earlier in my life...I don't believe that I would have been in this situation. If I had known that You were waiting for me to cry to You from a sincere heart...I would have done it years ago.

It's all my fault...not my father's!

Thank you Jesus!

Lazarus rise up…you are not dead!

U.S. District Judge Belot was removed from my case because of his outburst in the courtroom and I was reassigned to U.S. District Court Judge the Honorable J. Thomas Marten, who was considered the most lenient of the federal judges. Although I received a 48 months sentencing, it was much less than the 72 months that the U.S. prosecuting attorney was requesting.

FIVE
A Lesson of Survival

"And do not be conformed to this world, but be transformed by the renewing of your mind, that you may prove what is that good and acceptable and perfect will of God"

—*Romans 12:2*

I was sent to Yankton Federal Prison Camp in Yankton, South Dakota. I had never been to the state of South Dakota nor had any desire to visit the state, but now this would be the place that I called home for the next two years. It would have been a beautiful thing if I could have visited South Dakota without the memories of the two most challenging years of my life.

It's truly amazing where life will unexpectedly take you. I've learned after some tough experiences in my life to try to enjoy the scenery of the journey, because you may never pass that way again. So try to take it all in…the good and the bad!

From the time of my sentencing to arriving at Yankton Federal Prison Camp, about three months, the government made sure that I received my fair share of travel. They transferred me from one holding facility to another.

I never could understand why tax payers dollars where being spent on transferring prisoners weekly, instead of just sending you to where they were going to send you. You see, every time they had to transfer me, they had to send two U.S. Marshals to get me. This required time and money on the government's behalf, but I assumed they must have had the money to spend because I was moved pretty consistently every two weeks, from city to city. I even flew from Oklahoma City on "Con Air." I don't know if it was really called "Con Air" but when we entered the plane, we were shackled from head to toe and every time we landed the U.S. Marshals would surround the plane with guns just like the movie "Con Air."

When the shackles were placed on me, I immediately dropped my head in disgust...I was the second person in my family to enter and graduate from college. I was suppose to be one of the forerunners that would break this generational curse and charter a new path for our family, a path of success and prosperity...but I didn't...I failed not just myself, but my entire family.

I thought of all my forefathers about whom I had read who had fought and died over the years so that their future generations wouldn't have to be in shackles ever again. As I looked around this prison's holding facility, the majority of those in shackles looked like me... black like me. The slave trade all over again...caught and shipped to different plantations. Although this new slave owner didn't discriminate among the captives...it was all about the dollar bill. I couldn't help but think that somewhere up in heaven there were people watching me shaking their heads...thinking is this what we died for...what a waste of our blood, sweat and tears; thinking that they wish they had never cried to God to give them the strength to persevere for future generations to come...deep inside I cried from embarrassment.

Speaking of Oklahoma, it would be the last place I would visit before flying to Yankton, South Dakota and where I received my first lesson about prison life.

It would be in Oklahoma that I made the decision that regardless of how frighten I was inside; I would mask that feeling and put on this armor of "You Don't Know Me!"

In Ephesians 6: 14-16 it says "having girded your waist with truth, having put on the breastplate of righteousness, shod your feet with the preparation of the gospel of peace, and above all, taking the shield of faith with which you will be able to quench all the fiery darts of the wicked one." The Armor of God.

Well the "You Don't Know Me" armor is of toughness, seriousness and above all to look crazy, as if you're saying to all who are watching, and trust me…they're watching. If I have to kill someone…I will because I'm crazy.

I've never hurt anyone intentionally in my life…but I can truly say that during that period in my life that I would have. To survive I would have done whatever I had to do even if that meant to hurt, injure or kill another individual to protect myself I would have done it without giving it a second thought.

Like many of you, my knowledge of prison was what I had seen on television. Prison was a place that even the toughest of men get raped, stabbed, injured or even killed. I wasn't going to allow it to happen to me, if I could do something about it.

In Oklahoma, I met a man, with whom I often played chess, and who taught me the three most important rules you need to survive in prison. I believe that he shared this information with me because he could sense from outside my muscular body, that inside I was scared to death!

Maybe, he just wanted to pass this information to someone because no one ever passed it to him when he first went to prison.

Maybe this was his way of giving back to someone else which freed his conscience of wrong doing…I don't know but I am forever grateful.

You have to understand one thing before I proceed any further. Oklahoma is a destination point to which all inmates go before they are sent to their prison of confinement. When you're in Oklahoma, you don't know where you're actually going until you land at the assigned prison. People who have a familiarity with the prison system speculate where they will be assigned. The assignment is at the discretion of the prison board, not your high priced attorney, not even the Federal judge who sentenced you decides where you are sent. For security reasons, the prison board decides.

Rule 1... the most important rule of the three...Stay away from homosexuals! You don't want people to perceive that you get down like that... unless you do...in that case disregard this rule.

I don't personally have a problem with homosexuals because my oldest brother is a homosexual. He has been a protector of me and all of my other brothers and sisters, and I really could care less what you think of my brother...I love him...he's my brother... And I would die for him!

However, I understood this rule to the fullest...not a problem!

Rule 2...Stay out of the television rooms; they can quickly lead to trouble! Most fights that occur in prison stem from prisoners arguing over the television.

I struggled with this rule since I'm a sports guy and love watching all sports! Due to this fact...I would have several run-ins throughout my incarceration with other inmates. Just as he had warned me, I was unable to compromise with others concerning what we would be watching on the television.

Rule 3...Never discuss your case with anyone! You could be talking to an informant who would attempt to reduce their time by giving the federal government information about you and your case that came directly from your mouth.

I know, I know, I know...what your thinking. How can the federal government charge you with more crimes when they already have you incarcerated for a crime? I'm not an attorney but I do know first hand...that anything you say can and will be held against you in the court of law.

Relevant conduct... stuff I said out of fear and not facts...got me 48 months! Remember when I was crying in the courtroom...this was why...the government alleged that my statements had relevancy to my charge. I only had an ounce of powder cocaine in my house when they busted me but I spoke to the informant while wired, like I could purchase kilos of cocaine for him. I never did but the government charged me all the same.

All of this was going through my mind as I prepared to exit that plane that landed in Yankton, South Dakota.

How would I survive, could I make it behind these walls was what I was constantly questioning myself...didn't have a choice!

That reminded me of what I heard a judge tell an individual when I was in court waiting to be sentence. He'd ask the judge after sentencing...how do you expect me to do all this time to which you sentenced me?...the judge replied...Do what you can...even if you feel you can't do anymore...do what you can!!!!!

Do what I can...is that what this has come to!

Others don't know Lord...but I'm scared. I know that You have shown Yourself to be real in my life once I cried out to You...but I'm scared and I don't know what to expect once I arrive at this prison.

I can't and I repeat can't ...make it if I have to fight everyday for my survival behind prison walls. I couldn't take it if someone attempted to rape me...couldn't live with the shame. You have to do something Lord!

Lazarus you are not dead...rise up!

Thank you Lord for answering me...I'm afraid...I've never been to prison. This isn't jail where no one messes with you and you have your own cell to yourself...this is prison, Lord... guards with guns, large walls surrounded by barb-wire fences, inmates who are facing life in prison and men who wait for new inmates to arrive and to rape...prison, Lord.

Lazarus rise up...you are not dead!

"I will both lie down in peace, and sleep; For You alone, O Lord, make me dwell in safety." Psalm 4:8

Yankton Federal Prison Camp was a prison with no guards with guns, no walls, or barbwire fences. This prison was a beautiful former college campus that the federal government had purchased. It was surrounded by houses in the community. You could be a prisoner at Yankton Federal Prison Camp only if you had less than five years remaining on your sentence.

Thank you Lord...I can do this!

Six
If You Seek Wisdom...It Can Be Found

"Do not remember the former things, nor consider the things of old. Behold,
I will do a new thing."

—Isaiah 43: 18-19

"For as he thinks in his heart, so is he"

—Proverb 23:7

Prison is all about routine...once you find your routine then your days pass rapidly. My routine consisted of rising at 4:00 a.m., studying and conversing with God about things I had read in His Word. I use to challenge myself by writing a Bible verse that spoke to me everyday. Then I would go over these verses daily. Before I stopped... I was reciting about 100 Bible verses daily.

"Seek first the kingdom of God and His righteousness, and all these things shall be added to you." Matthew 6:33

I would walk to breakfast with my friend DP, who was from Gary, Indiana, around 6:30 a.m. The conversations we had were mind blowing. DP was my spiritual brother, who was seeking answers from God like I was.

DP did not go to college. He dropped out of high school to sell drugs, because in his opinion that's what everyone in Gary, Indiana did. DP said that everyone was trying to leave Gary, and the only way that they thought they could was through selling drugs.

Wait…isn't Gary home to Michael Jackson? Yep…it's also one of the most impoverished cities in the United States.

DP never knew that I envied him…he was 23 years old, and as smart as any person that I had met in my college days but more importantly…he was the most disciplined person that I had ever, and I mean ever met. DP read every book that was written about how to become successful and he implemented a plan to not spend any of the money that he would acquire from his job while incarcerated.

Outside of the cafeteria, DP only ate Ramen Noodles and would encourage his girlfriend from home, with whom had three children not to spend any of the government assistance money she was receiving until he came home in two years. DP wanted the children to eat the way he was eating…only Ramen Noodles, with meat added occasionally; to not have any new clothes or shoes…DP said everyone would have to sacrifice because he had a plan to make money "flipping houses" when he returned to Gary.

As crazy as this may seem…DP was serious and would argue with his girlfriend constantly when she would inform him that she had to spend money on anything…like food, clothes, shoes just to mention a few things that kids need. Don't let her call him and say that she had purchased anything new for herself…DP wasn't having it!

Nevertheless, I loved DP, and I admired his discipline and dedication. We both grew leaps and bounds in God's Word. We challenged each other to have uncompromising faith to do the unthinkable. Like the story of Paul and Silas in prison…

But at midnight Paul and Silas were praying and singing hymns to God, and the prisoners were listening to them. Suddenly there was a great earthquake, so that the foundations of the prison were shaken; and immediately all the doors were opened and everyone's chains were loosed. Acts 16:25-26

DP use to say to me every night before I went to sleep that once I awaken, that he was not going to be there. He would say that because God had pardoned him, no prison could hold him…real, unthinkable faith.

I, on the other hand, didn't want my friend to go…didn't touch and agree with him in my heart, but would give him assurance with my mouth that I was in agreement…Selfish…I know, but I needed my friend and I knew whatever the two of us would agree …God would perform!

So I would respond…DP, the federal government calls what your talking about escape and it carries with it an additional 24 months …so keep yourself in this room!

This was every day…

After returning to the room from breakfast, I would challenge the other nine men in the room that I shared to explain the new word that I discovered in my reading at 4:00 a.m. that morning.

In federal prison, everyone gets counted at the same time across the nation. Census count at 8:00 a.m., 12:00 p.m. and 4:00 p.m., …everyone who can stand is standing getting counted by the guards everyday Sunday through Saturday. No exception; so, even if you don't choose to go to breakfast, you still have to stand at 8:00 a.m.to be counted.

I'm a morning person so no problem…

This vocabulary word challenge kept my mind sharp, and it gave me some insight with whom I was sharing my living quarters. Two men, Cali and Q had pretty high I.Qs. This exercise was challenging to them to see which one could give the definition. Cali, a Muslim brother around my age was from Compton, California. He would always be the first to attempt to define the word. More often than not he would be correct. I enjoyed the bantering that took place between us.

Our differences in what we believed was the foundation of a respectful relationship. I was a Christian and Cali was a Muslim. In prison usually everyone keeps the company of those who share similar beliefs. However, God allowed me, because of my heart, to walk in Love…if God is love, then I believed that the best way I could exemplify God's love would be to be friendly to everyone and to show compassion to all regardless of what they believed.

I'm not talking about compromising my own beliefs but to show that Agape kind of love to all. We were already locked up together...We didn't have to fight each other just because one believed something different from what another believed? If it's God...it will keep... and God doesn't need me to defend Him or His Word...so Cali was a friend.

Q was an older white attorney about 6"3" from East St. Louis...this man was the most intelligent man I have ever known in my life. His mastery of the English vocabulary astonished me. Q never missed defining a vocabulary word and he would even use the word in a sentence. It frustrated me greatly that I could never stump Q with any word in my Webster's Dictionary.

Q hated the federal government with every inch of his being...his only goal was to stick it to the federal government any chance that he could. He had owned a newspaper in East St. Louis and would frequently comment about the corruption within the federal government. This lead to the federal governments pursuit of Q...and they caught him.

His appeals attorney was Shapiro...yep the attorney on the O.J. Simpson case...promise...I even got the opportunity to meet Shapiro.

I use to try to persuade Q to let all that hatred go and move on but he wouldn't...couldn't ...felt the government cost him too much. I use to share with Q how God commands us to forgive, even though Q was a non believer, he liked me and would talk about his case with me.

Remember earlier when I mentioned the three rules to survive in prison...rule three... never discuss your case with anyone...Q broke this rule because he would say that I reminded him of his son...I had faith in something in which he had lost faith.

He once told me that he would be willing to review my case because he believed that I received a raw deal...I told Q...thank you but no thanks!

I'm afraid of the federal government...I've seen first hand what they can do when they set their minds to it...so no thanks, I don't want anything to do with the federal government except getting my release papers.

He responded by telling me how the government offered him a plea agreement of no jail time, but he would lose his license to practice law, if he would just accept guilt for something which he said he was innocent...he refused and told me that he couldn't accept guilt for something which he said he was innocent. How would he have the courage to look upon his son after that...and I quote, "I would rather kiss my own behind and then shoot myself in the head!"

Wow...I told him...I could...if it would have kept me from going to prison!

His response to me was...then where is this faith that you have been preaching to me ...if you don't stand for something then you will fall for anything!

Sometimes...you should keep your mouth closed because once you open it, you let the world know who you are...

His words would later give me strength in my battle to believe God at His Word and to stand when everything around me is telling me to tuck tail and run.

As I'm writing this book, I realize that God used three different men to mold me into the person that I am today. He used a man who had not finished high school (a drop out), a man who practiced a different faith than I do (Muslim), and a man who didn't believe in anything but his own ability (Atheist).

They were all good men who had come to the same place at an appointed time...they would be my Wise Men who came to my birth (understanding of God's Word) to shower me with gifts (knowledge/ information) that I would take and apply to my life.

You can learn something from anyone if you're open and thirsting for knowledge!

"A wise man will hear and increase learning, And a man of understanding will attain wise counsel." Proverb 1:5

In prison everyone is responsible for having a job. Isn't it ironic the government can provide employment for everyone who is incarcerated but on the outside employment can be difficult to obtain.

I had several jobs throughout my two years of incarceration; a certified dental assistant; an employee of the local marina, and my favorite job was working for the Army Reserves Armory. At this job I met my future mentor GK, or Sgt.

GK was from St. Louis and had been a distinguished police Sergeant, whose crime was "double dipping." The federal government convicted GK on taking money from two jobs while only working at one job site? Basically, the government alleged that GK got paid from his second job without working the hours of the second job.

It would be at the Armory that GK and I spent countless hours talking about everything from faith, politics, women, education and my favorite...sports! GK was an avid St. Louis Rams fan...this just happened to be the time that the St. Louis Rams were good... so I could never get him to stop talking about those St. Louis Rams.

I use to wonder if GK was a Rams fan when the team was horrible...he would say...once a fan always a fan!

I'm sure some of you are wondering how we were working outside the prison...well let explain.

As I said earlier, everyone in federal prison has to have a job. These jobs pay from $0.20 to $3.00 an hour. If you're making $3.00 an hour, then you have just completed one of the federal apprentice programs. Most inmates are attempting to survive on about $1.25 an hour. This is why it is critical that you have friends, or family support.

Most prisoners who are incarcerated these days are incarcerated for selling and distributing drugs. These men were supporting entire families before they were incarcerated...Now how they supported their families by selling drugs was wrong...lets not pretend that it's not. Selling drugs not only ruins families but it ruins communities. People make wrong decisions when faced with adversity...despite the consequences.

Survival will always out weigh good judgment...

I was blessed and I truly mean blessed that Danuyell took care of me financially. Others were less fortunate...they had no one to send them money on a weekly or monthly basis. I on the other hand, had Danuyell send me $200.00 every month for two years, and my mother would send what she could...how blessed was that...I can't thank them enough, even if I try.

Jobs are important because as I describe previously this is the only income for 75% of all prisoners. Big ballers out in the world...but broke in prison, with no one to send them anything...Their well has gone dry!

For some inmates, working in the community for free is an option once you're sentence is below one year from your release. I couldn't wait...and once it became an option for me...I took it and ran. I didn't need the money because I had Danuyell...working outside the prison allowed God to show me that this time would eventually pass, because I was working for good men in the Armory.

These Army Reserve officers didn't treat me or GK like we were prisoners but like employees of the Army Reserve. You can't imagine how good it felt to be treated like a man and not a prisoner...I have all the respect in the world for those men, they didn't have to treat us the way they did.

Reflecting on the situation...I can see God at work...He freed me of hatred; hatred of everyone that I blamed for my situation; hatred of everyone who didn't write me to check to see how I was doing. God had his hand on me and He was speaking to my situation like He spoke toward Job when all hell was breaking out in Job's life...

And the Lord said to Satan, "Behold, all that he has is in your power; only do not lay a hand on his person." Job 1:12

You can cause all hell to break out around him...but you can't kill him!

I needed men like GK and those officers at the Armory...because sometimes strength is hard to find even if you have faith while you're in prison...but it would be men like GK who would help me find my inner strength to persevere and find contentment in my present state.

"For I have learned in whatever state I am, to be content" Philippians 4:11

Now, I don't ever want to give the impression that I'm disrespecting my father, but GK was everything that I always said I wanted in a father. He imparted wisdom into me, he spoke blessings over me and would demand that when I left prison that I take my rightful place in society and make a contribution...he would say to me...No Excuses!

After seven years, we still maintain close contact...I love GK.

After work, there is a census count and then the most important part of the day...mail.

I can't begin to explain to those who have never been incarcerated the importance of an inmate receiving mail. This and this alone could be the determination of how an inmate will serve his incarceration. Those who receive mail weekly, and I'm suggesting one letter a week, usually have a smoother transition then those who never receive mail.

Mail to a person who is locked up signifies whether or not that person is being missed by family or loves ones. When you don't get mail, you feel as if no one loves you or even cares...those are feelings of depression...suicide.

It is only human to desire to be loved and cared about...without that, what do you have? What reason do you have to live...now don't get me wrong, I know some men incarcerated were evil men and those that they hurt couldn't wait for those men to go away...but even those men need and desire love.

In this area, God would use Danuyell to provide for me more than I could ever imagine...truth be told...much more than I deserved.

My mother wrote me twice a month...thank you Momma...I love you. Danuyell. wrote me every day for two years...I'm not kidding...seven days a week for two years, I received a letter from Danuyell...I didn't deserve her or her acts of love and compassion..

Her treatment to me was out of the ordinary as I observed the prisoners at Yankton.

This was my routine for two years...God sent people in my life to free me from hatred, anger, loneliness and worry...I could focus on having intimacy with my Creator.

Lazarus you are not dead...rise up!

Lord, I know Your voice now...what would You have me to do?

Lazarus rise up...you are not dead!

"A word in season to him...who is weary."Isaiah 50:4

SEVEN
What Am I Going to Do Now?

"Be anxious for nothing, but in everything by prayer and supplication, with thanksgiving, let your requests be made known to God; and the peace of God, which surpasses all understanding, will guard your hearts and minds through Christ Jesus."

—Philippians 4:6-7

The remainder of my days were spent listening and studying God's Word...I listened and watched tapes of speakers like Joyce Meyer, who taught me how the battle was being fought in my mind...Rob Parsley, who is a white minister but if you hear him, you would swear he was black minister, this man could preach, and Pastor Parsley really seem to me to have a heart for all people of all races...I liked Parsley. Creflo Dollar who taught about prosperity...my kind of teaching...which was totally different from what I had learned attending church.

You mean to tell me that God doesn't want me to be broke, that he desires to bless me financially...I couldn't stop listening to this man, Creflo Dollar...and besides...I'm love his last name...Dollar.

My favorite pastor was T.D. Jakes. I loved listening to his sermons...he actually had tapes for prisoners to listen and watch his videos. DP and I probably watched his "Man Power" tapes over a hundred times…yes, we even watched his tapes on "Women Thou Are Loose" but it was something about the way Bishop Jakes spoke to men about real life situations that they were facing. He had applied God's Word to these situations.

DP and I would promised each other that one day we, too, would be at "Man Power" and get an opportunity to meet Bishop Jakes to tell him just how much his teaching helped us…I promise …I will be there…have to be there.

Because God had been blessing me with peace of mind and assuring me that everything would be okay…I did something that I never had done …I tithed.

Tithing was a big deal for me. I didn't think that the money I was giving was going to God…I thought it was going to the pastor, who seem to be doing better than I was, so he didn't need my little money anyway. Tithing was something bigger now…it wasn't about any pastor receiving my money, but my way of saying…Thank You God!…I know that I'm still locked up …but **as I look back over these last two years**…You have been faithful and so good to me that I want to **Bless You God** and do something for You. So the money that I'm going to send…I ask You God to receive…I know that I can never repay you for all the times You have been there for me; college; the classroom; the courtroom; in the jail cell; and now here in Yankton, but this is my way of saying thank you for showing grace and mercy toward a sinner like me who wasn't even thinking about You while You were always thinking about me.

I sent 10% of all the checks that Danuyell had saved of from my teaching contract, which the Wichita Public Schools paid me from February to June. That was a big sacrifice for me… since I would be leaving here…in three months…I would need all of my money, so to give 10% was a big deal for me.

I wrote Bishop Jakes and Creflo Dollar letters explaining how through their ministry I had been blessed and that I wanted to plant a seed of faith by tithing…a leap of faith for me.

It felt good for once to be obedient to one of God's principals…yes, I think I can make it…I don't have a choice…no excuses!

My days at Yankton were coming to an end... I begin to think about my life and how I would support myself upon my return to Wichita, Kansas.

For me...I struggled with whether or not I would be allowed to teach again and if I couldn't teach then what would I do?

A very frightening thought that one would have with oneself, who is in prison, ...the thought of **what am I going to do now**.

I guarantee you that every prisoner has this personal conversation at some point...

Once you get over thinking about all you're going to do with family and friends, who never wrote you, you start thinking......**what am I going to do now.**

Because the world didn't stop once you went away...it continued turning upon its axis and people continued living...the only thing that stopped was you...and you didn't really stop; you were just isolated from society... Its like you were placed in time-out for an extended time.

Lord, what am I going to do now?

Lazarus ...Be anxious for nothing!

I hear you Lord...but the media has reported that I will never teach again and if I can't teach then what will I do?

Lazarus...If I, God Almighty be for you...then who can be against you!

But Lord...the people here in prison in my required exit classes are telling me that once I complete an application, I should check the box that indicated that I've been incarcerated...won't that automatically disqualify me for any position ...I don't want to lie but why can't I leave it blank and address it in the interview...that would at least gives me a chance to explain myself and my situation.

Lazarus...have I not commanded you to be strong...I am with you where ever you go.

It would be during this time that God would show me a vision...a vision of me speaking in front of millions of people...teaching young men how to avoid the mistakes that I had made in life so that they would not end up in a similar situation.

When you receive a vision that you know is from God…it can be overwhelming. In your mind, you begin to wonder if you can fulfill this enormous calling… you begin to doubt yourself and whether or not you have what it takes … you even start questioning if it were God who spoke to you in this vision.

Those questions were going through my mind…I was looking at my situation and what others, in particular the media had said about me. I doubted if God could restore me…to be honest…if God wanted to restore me. I knew that God had forgiven me and I believed that I had forgiven myself…but how, where and when would I teach again was all that I wanted to know…God had shown me a vision that seem to correspond with the desire of my heart…I had no idea of what it would cost me to achieve this vision.

EIGHT
Why Me?...Why Now?

"For a righteous man may fall seven times And rise again"
—Proverbs 24:16

I was released from prison on January 16, 2001. After spending two years and ten months of my life behind bars, I left with mixed emotions about what I would now do with my life. Being locked up for those two years was somewhat easy in the sense that I didn't have any responsibilities. Don't get me wrong, I hated being away from the people that I loved , but prison had preserved me. I hadn't been to any night clubs, hadn't had any alcohol to drink or hadn't been sexually active with any woman for over two years. I read constantly every book that was placed in front of me...from spiritual to financial to practical books. Now I had to make a living for myself.

I was released to the federal halfway house six months early, and was assigned to a federal probation officer, and their only objective for me was that I had to obtain a job...soon...no exceptions!

I applied for teaching jobs in other states, believing God would answer my prayer of teaching again...He would... but not the way that I had envisioned it.

I received a call from a Principal of a Montessori school in Baltimore, Maryland one week after I was released asking me if I would be interested in coming to Maryland to interview for a middle school teaching job...the school would pay for all the arrangements if I agreed.

Thank you God...You are faithful to Your word...I agreed to go to Baltimore Maryland.

The only problem that I potentially saw was how my probation officer would agree to this in such a short notice...the rule was that she, the probation officer, needed at least three weeks notice to confirm everything through clearance. This was a problem because the principal in Baltimore needed a math teacher now...within the next week or she would have to find someone else to fill the position.

What was I going to do...God had opened a door for me...I believed...but...I would have to break the rules and go to Baltimore without my probation officer knowing...what would you do?...I went to Baltimore without informing my probation officer.

This choice could have had a number of negative consequences for me. I could have been sent back to prison to finish the remainder of my sentence or better yet...the government could have given me more time to serve...but I felt I had to take the risk...this was an answer to my prayer ...to be given an opportunity to teach again.

Once I arrived in Baltimore, I shared with the principal my situation...I was honest and this African American lady was willing to give me a chance...she even said that I could stay in her basement until I found a place to live. Her only request was that I wasn't on drugs...I assured her that I was only involved in the distribution of drugs; I did not consumed them.

She said that she understood that people make mistakes and that everyone deserves a second chance because she herself had a son my age that was addicted to drugs. She wished that she could help him but she didn't know what else to do for her him after time and money spent in numerous rehab centers.

Her only request was for me to assure her that I had not used drugs...once again, I assured her that I had never used drugs other than marijuana maybe ten times in my entire adulthood life.

I told her that my probation officer would be calling her to verify my employment opportunity and that I wasn't suppose to be in Baltimore because I didn't get permission from her …so I needed her, the principal to act as if she offered me the job as the result of a phone interview.

You don't have to tell me that I was wrong…but what was I suppose to do when the probation officer wasn't going to let me go to Baltimore?

The principal agreed…however, she said that the probation officer would need to contact her within the next three days because she was going on vacation and would not be in the school until a week or so later……also, she didn't want to inform her assistant principal about my situation…she said no one else needed to know ….I agreed!

I returned home and called my probation officer informing her that I had a job offer to teach in Baltimore, Maryland and that I had a place to stay when I got to Baltimore. I asked her if she could call the number of the principal within the next three days because the principal would be leaving in three days…my probation officer said that she would, but questioned how I was given a job opportunity over the phone so quickly upon my release from prison…she also wanted to know if this principal was informed of my drug conviction and that I had just been released from prison.

I assured her that the principal had been informed of all the circumstances surrounding my incarceration, and the principal still wanted to hire me as a teacher and was willing to let me use her residence until I was able to pay for my own.

My probation officer called five days later and spoke to the assistant principal and told the assistant principal that once I relocated to Baltimore Maryland, I would be required to undergo drug counseling because of my drug conviction. The assistant principal told my probation officer that she was unaware that I would have to attend drug counseling and that she didn't know if the principal was informed of this counseling requirement.

I received a call a week later from the principal informing me that I would not be receiving a teaching position with the Montessori Middle School in Baltimore, Maryland…she was crying on the phone while she was explaining to me that she would not be able to justify to her administrative staff why I had to attend drug counseling.

I told her that my probation officer requires all of her clients who have drug convictions to attend drug counseling...it was her requirement.

The principal said that the probation officer had made it appear to her assistant principal that I had to take this drug counseling course because I had a drug addiction not because I had a drug offense.

I cried and told the principal...thank you for the opportunity and I was sorry that she couldn't hire me...she cried like a mother who had to say goodbye to a son that she would never see again!!!

Lord...why, why, why does this always have to happen to me...You promised that I would teach again...why did my probation officer have to do me like this...she knew that I didn't need any drug counseling and on top of that...she said she would call the principal within three days...she waited five...why, why, why!!!

Lazarus...So shall My word be that goes forth from My mouth; It shall not return to Me void, But it shall accomplish what I please, And it shall prosper in the thing for which I sent it. Isaiah 55:11

I hear you Lord but it hurts terribly to be disappointed...to have hope in something only to see it shattered right in front of my face...it hurts Lord.

Lazarus...I'm with you where ever you go... and My word will accomplish what I please and will not return to Me void.

It took me a couple days to get over that disappointment...but the federal government is not in the business of waiting...I had to find a job and find it now.

Pepsi Bottling Company was hosting a job fair. Everyone who was looking for a job, if they had a resume was instructed to bring it at 7:00 p.m. that evening.

I was there at exactly 7:00 p.m. and the doors were closed to everyone...disappointment once again...the president of Pepsi Bottling Company came to the door apologizing to everyone saying that Pepsi didn't expect this type of a response. They would have another job fair in the near future and all of us should watch for it...by the way...he said that if anyone had their resume he would take it and give it to the appropriate staff member.

I handed the president of Pepsi Bottling Company my resume...feeling disappointed that I wasn't afforded the opportunity to interview with those who were in the fair...I received a call the next day...I promise on everything, the next day... I'm not exaggerating...the next day...offering me a job as an Account Manager Trainee...I never interviewed for any job with Pepsi...Pepsi offered me the job because the president of Pepsi recommended me for the Account Manager Trainee position.

Thank you Lord...just when I think that You have forgotten about me...a miracle occurs...thank you, thank you...Your awesome and faithful to Your word.

NINE
Kansas City, Here I Come

"I'm going to Kansas City…Kansas City here I come"
—Roy Drusky

"I will bring the blind by a way they did not know; I will lead them in paths they have not known. I will make darkness light before them. And crooked places straight. These things I will do for Lazarus, And not forsake Lazarus."
—Isaiah 42:16

I worked at Pepsi Bottling Company for almost two years. An account manager is the person who comes and organizes pop displays in grocery stores. The manager also has to sell or convince grocery store managers that Pepsi deserves front display rather than Coke…but to be honest both Coke and Pepsi have contracts with most grocery stores. That means that both Coke and Pepsi alternate which pop is on sale that week…if you don't believe me, the next time your in a grocery store…look and see what the cost is of Pepsi and Coke. They will rarely be the same price…one will always be priced lower than the other…except during holidays…both Pepsi and Coke will be priced same.

I don't want to sound ungrateful, because I was extremely grateful to have a job that paid pretty well with excellent benefits…but my heart wasn't in it.

I was making a living working at Pepsi, like a lot of people who make their living at Pepsi, but I yearned for my first love…teaching. Oh…how I missed her. If only she would give me another chance…I promise this time to never cheat on her with anyone…I would forsake all others…just to have her back in my life one more time.

Psalm 37:4 says…"Delight yourself also in the Lord, And He shall give you the desires of your heart"…well, my desire was teaching and I needed God to move because this account manager business was killing me my spirit.

Danuyell, the person with whom I had been living since my return from prison, was going to a conference in Kansas City. She encouraged me to go to Kansas City with her as she often did. Free vacation…My brother Calvin, the first college graduate in our family, was living in Kansas City. I called Calvin to inform him that Danuyell and I would be coming to Kansas City for one of her conferences and that I wanted to see him. I love my brother and hadn't seen him since he had visited me at the prison in Yankton, South Dakota.

Once, I arrived in Kansas City, Calvin started asking me the usual…how are things going…do you need anything…what's up with you and Danuyell, whom he really liked. Calvin started talking about one of his fraternity brothers who was a principal in Kansas City. He wanted me to meet this fraternity brother.

Let me explain a couple of things at this point…first, I want to acknowledge all of my brothers whom I have not mentioned until this point…I love all of my brothers, Troynell, Tyrone, Shawn (my brother-in-law, who is my hero) and Scotty……but Calvin is the brother to whom I'm the closest because we are separated by ten months in birth.

My mother used to dress us as twins in school because our birthdays were so close. The only difference between us was that Calvin was light-skinned and I was dark-skinned.

My dark-skin would be an internal conflict with which I would struggle for years…even as an adult…because it would be my dark-skin that I attributed my grandmother's unfair treatment toward me. If you recall, I mentioned my grandmother would give one of us...Calvin, a present for Christmas, his birthdays and graduations. When it came to me, she would say that she was sorry...but she forgot me...that she would get me later. I honestly thought that she loved my brother more than me only because Calvin was light-skinned and I was dark-skinned. Because everyone else said that we looked alike... what else could there have been...but my dark-skin that kept my grandmother from loving me like she loved Calvin.

What I loved about Calvin was that every time my Grandmother would give him a gift right in front of me...while I walked off to..."I'm sorry I forgot you but will get you something later"...Calvin would find me outside trying to hold back my tears...and he would say to me that because he was my older brother and that he loved me that he didn't want his gift from grandma...something I believe my father should have said. Because of this situation, Calvin left grandma's house without his gift...I truly believed that he would return and get the gift later because the gift always had a funny way of finding its way back to our house...but it meant the world to me that Calvin would do that for me...he knew how badly I was hurting inside.

I struggled with my dark-skin for years...I didn't think that anyone could love me because of it. The irony to this dilemma is that our father has dark-skin like mine and not light-skin like Calvin...if anyone should have understood the complexities of being dark-skinned in America, my father should have. Maybe that was why he never interfered with my grandma's treatment of me... because he never felt loved; to have at least one of his children receive the love that he should have received as a child was enough to him...maybe he thought that my grandmother wasn't doing any more to me than what she did to him ...he saw strength in me that I could take it...like he took it...maybe...who knows...but it took me years to be comfortable in my dark-skin and at 37 years old I'm just now starting to think...this dark-skin is cooooool...it does have some advantages in this life...and besides, no matter how much Ambie cream I use...this dark-skin is here to stay...so love it.

Okay…back to the story…Calvin and I were extremely close but every time we would get together, we were always competing…sports, women, clothes, education, and my favorite…fraternities.

Calvin's fraternity is the fraternity that dresses in red and white, twirling canes around only wishing but knowing in their heart that they are not worthy to wear the colors of my fraternity whose members dressed in purple and wore gold boots…as you can see the saga continues.

When Calvin started talking about his fraternity brother who was a principal…I immediately starting thinking about any fraternity brothers of mine who where principals…just in case I had to one up him…but Calvin surprised me by saying that he could mention me to his fraternity brother and possible get me a job in Kansas City teaching…I told Calvin…make it happen.

Lord…it's me again…could this be true…could I actually teach once more…You did promise me Lord that I would teach again…but if this is not it…please don't let me go to Kansas City to accept a teaching job only at the last moment to have it taken away from me…I can't accept disappointment…not right now… I would rather stay in Wichita, Kansas where things are convenient……than to take a leap of faith and face rejection and disappointment.

Lazarus…I will establish My Word in you…and I will perform it.

I hear you Lord…but I can't have another situation like I had in Baltimore, Maryland…not with teaching…I love her too much to have to experience another disappointment…it took a lot out of me…but Lord…

Lazarus rise up…I will never leave you nor forsake you…I will be with you where ever you go.

His fraternity brother called me that next week offering me a job to teach freshman math and coach football at Westport High School in Kansas City, Missouri. He offered me the same salary that I was making at Pepsi Bottling Company…$36,000.00…and I had a place to live…with Calvin…all I had to do was move to Kansas City…which meant the end of my relationship with Danuyell.

Danuyell…I could write an entire book about how great, intelligent, beautiful, friendly and loyal of a woman she is and was for me…but that is not this story… I will just ask God to **bless Danuyell a hundred fold** for what she did for me. If it weren't for Danuyell there probably would not be a book…at least the story would not be the same…so thank you Lord for sending me an angel…I will never forget you!

TEN
Finding My Church Home

"The life that you are living is a direct result of the words that were spoken over you. If you don't like your life then change your confession."
–Dr. Steve Houpe
Harvest Church
January 19, 2005

"He who finds a wife finds a good thing. And obtains favor from the Lord."
–Proverbs 18:22

I moved to Kansas City in July of 2002 after accepting the teaching job at Westport High School. I thought that everything was going according to God's plan for my life...God had fulfilled a promise He made while I was in prison that I would teach again ...until that ugly demon, called my past, would surface and again ruin everything.

It wasn't even a full three months when the principal called me into his office to inform me that Edison, who sponsored Westport High School was requiring me to have my certification in order to continue teaching at the school .

A couple of things...first, I lost my license while I was incarcerated and I had no way to plea my case before the state board because I was unaware that my license was being revoked. Secondly, when I was arrested, the middle school where I taught at was an Edison school…and they still remembered.

Lord…why, why, why, why do I have to always have to fight for something…I asked you Lord that if this was going to be another Baltimore, Maryland situation to let me stay in Wichita where everything was cool…but no…You sent me to Kansas City and now they're threatening to remove me from the classroom because my Kansas license was revoked.

Lazarus…I'm with you where ever you go.

I submitted my application to the Missouri Department of Education for my teaching license and the Missouri Department of Education did something that it had informed me that it had never done…**IT TOOK NO ACTION!**

Took no action was just three words which meant that the State Board of Education of Missouri, will not deny you your license, but will not grant you a teacher's license at this time…to me…it meant No license…no job.

Lord…what am I going to do now…I'm in Kansas City without a job now…I've got to do something…I can't go back to Wichita because it would be a constant reminder of my failures in my past…you have to move somehow on my situation.

Lazarus…I'm not moved by emotions…I'm moved by My Word…If I spoke it I'm well able to bring it to perform it.

I receive a permanent 7th grade math substitute teaching job with the Kansas City Missouri School District…a district that to this day can't explain why they hired me without either a teaching certificate or substitute teaching certificate.

Fine with me…I had a job to finish the year…and I believed that I could find another teaching job before the next school year started…thank you Lord.

This was the time in my life that I would find a new church home…like everything else that had happened in my life, finding Harvest Church happened when I needed it the most.

I remember getting my hair cut at the barber shop and being handed this brochure about a Man's Conference that was coming to a church called Harvest in Kansas City. To be honest, I wouldn't have thought anything about it but the brochure had as one of it's guest speakers...Deion Sanders...the football player for whom I have the most respect.

I had never been to any conference...let alone a Christian conference. My definition of church was Sunday and maybe Wednesday for bible study...but I never socialized with any men I thought were Christians...maybe, because I never viewed Christians as people who have fun. They were people, in my opinion, who attempted to force feed you the word of God by always telling you what you were doing wrong and never what they were doing wrong...fake people...and I don't do fake.

One problem, I didn't have anyone with whom to attend this conference. Few men go anywhere by themselves.

As fate would have it...I couldn't find anyone and my brother was busy that night...so I went by myself.

First of all Harvest Church is a long way north by Worlds of Fun. The length of the drive almost made me stop but I continued. Once I was there, my first thought was that this must be one of those mega churches because it is huge. This church was once a mall that had been converted into a church...grandiose. I get into the doors and men are greeting me with "God Bless You Brother" shaking my hand left and right. Just to get into the conference...I promise I must have shaken at least ten brothers hands...and about three brothers had embraced me in a hug fashion...weird...but comforting feeling occurred inside me...a feeling of...I love you Brother as a man of God, even though I don't know you...I love you.

Once inside the conference...hundreds of men are yelling and crying "thank you God"...I remembered crying to God in that jail cell before sentencing...but I was by myself, even though that night it wouldn't have mattered who saw me, I needed God...but these men of all races were doing it openly...Wow...is all that I could say...maybe some of these men had been through situations similar to mine, was all I could think

...because in my life the only people I had ever seen cry to God openly were women...and the tapes of men I had seen of T.D. Jakes "ManPower" where men were doing this very same crying out loud to God.

Deion Sanders speaks and gives his testimony about football, women, and giving his life to Christ. It was really cool... but it was this man whom they called Pastor Steve Houpe that would rock my foundation.

This Pastor started talking about fathers and lack of fathers in a man's life. How at a young age he and his father were extremely poor, and how he came home one day from school to find his father dead...he said that regardless of how tough his father was on him, it was his father who had taken care of him, and now that man lay dead right before him...and I thought I had it rough.

He continued talking for about an hour...then he said to the congregation of men...that God had called him on behalf of all the fathers in that room to say to their sons...I love you. By this time as you could imagine...all the men in the conference were crying...and I mean boo-whooing crying. Pastor Houpe proceeded around the room and hugged every man and told him ...You're going to make it...I love you.

When he approached me...he said something different...he said that he knew by the Spirit of God that God had called me to his church to be by his side...double Wow...I'm crying like a baby in his presence, tears flying everywhere and he grabs me by my face and wipes away the tears and says to me...You're going to make it...I love you son.

I met many men in this church that weren't fake...men that faced everyday issues just like me but were believing and relying on God as their source of survival. It was because of Pastor Houpe and the men of Harvest that I attended "Man-Power" in Atlanta Georgia.

I had prayed to God in prison for an example of a good man after whom I could model and God had answered my prayers by sending me to Dr. Steve Houpe of Harvest Church in Kansas City, Missouri...I'm not saying that this man is perfect...and I don't place him on a pedestal... but Dr. Houpe is honest about his own personal struggles from which God has delivered him...I like that...a Pastor who is transparent...but for me...he called me son...and I believe in all of my heart that he meant it. This man is the only man that when I'm in his presence...I can be the young, innocent Terrance who isn't afraid of being hurt or scared of anything because I know he won't allow anything to hurt me…a father's love for a son.

It was at Harvest Church that I would met my lovely wife, Christina Williams. We met and were married four months later. She would be the vessel that God used to pour strength into me, when I felt like quitting. I can't begin to tell you how many days and nights she would be on her face crying to God for me to take my rightful place. Because although we were married…the old me that enjoyed running around with women, drinking and living ungodly would have to die to really enjoy all that God would have me to accomplish in this life.

Its tough man…I know…but a praying woman is powerful. Especially, a woman who is humble enough to show other women out of her hurt how to pray…that's powerful.

My life was going pretty well at this point…I was teaching math and was the Athletic Director at Faith Academy, which is apart of Harvest Church…I had a church home and a spiritual father who loved me like a son…I was married…. I had just started working toward my master's degree in Educational Administration…hoping to one day become a Principal…life was okay…the only storms in my life seem to be the ones that I cause.

Lord…it's me again. I know that I'm not at a traditional school but I am teaching even if it's in a parochial school…I'm teaching again. But I need you to help me because I'm about to lose my wife because I don't know how to be a husband…I've never seen a faithful husband. Teach me Lord, because beginning again takes too much time and energy…and You Lord have given me a good woman…I just need to be shown how to be good to her…show me Lord…teach me.

Lazarus…honor your wife that your prayers may not be hindered.

Lord…I don't know how…show me.

Lazarus…I will be with you where every you go…and I have given you a man to show you My ways.

I would, however, get a divorce, after two years of marriage, after the birth of my son…I, also, left Harvest Church…but my heart continued to stay with my spiritual father, Dr. Steve Houpe.

ELEVEN

No Greater Joy than the Birth of My Son

"And the younger of them said to his father, 'Father, give me the portion of goods that falls to me.' So he divided to them the livelihood. And not many days after, the younger son gathered all together, journeyed to a far country, and there wasted his possessions with prodigal living."
–Luke 15:12-13

Honor your wife that your prayers may not be hindered…what would hindered prayers look like Lord…I don't want my prayers hindered but I don't think that my wife and I are going to make it…I know Lord that you gave her to me but we're two totally different people and if she can't see it my way…then, it's not going to work.

For the next several years of my life…nothing would go right. After having my teaching license denied from the Missouri Department of Education, I decided to go back to the Kansas Department of Education seeking the reinstatement of my teaching license since Kansas was where the crime was committed. I was lead to believe that if Kansas would reissue me my teaching license, then Missouri would also grant me a license…but Kansas would deny me my license for four straight years…nothing went right, there was failure and disappointment time and time again.

For four years straight I would appear before the Kansas Professional Practices Commission for my teaching license. The commission would require me to present evidence at the hearing to demonstrate the nature and seriousness of my conduct that resulted in the revocation of my license is no longer a factor in my fitness to engage in the profession of teaching and school administration.

I would do just that …and each time the members would vote not to reissue my license at that time. For four years straight their verdict was always the same…they couldn't get past the seriousness of the crime. The one factor of my conviction that I couldn't change was the seriousness!

Although I was eligible under the law to have my license reissued…the Practicing Commission continued to deny me on the premise of not enough time had elapse from the crime being committed. On my third appearance before The Practicing Commission they actually said to me, "Mr. Vick you no longer need to present any further information pertaining to what you have done the past three years to demonstrate that your past behavior ceases to exist."…but they still denied me.

Lord…what more can I do…I have done everything that the Practicing Commission asked me to do… I'm teaching at a school without a license, at a salary much lower than what my education and experience should command…I've been accepted into Park University graduate school to receive my master's degree in Administration of Education …I have a 4.0 in the classes that I have taken… I've had no trouble with the law, with the exception of a speeding violation… everything that the Practicing Commission has asked of me, I've done…but yet they still deny me……I don't know what else I can do…..and yes, for those who may be thinking……I hired an attorney the fourth time I appeared before the Practicing Commission to see if the attorney could help me get my license reissued…the answer was still the same…no…not at this time!

The attorney would later tell me that the state of Kansas had never reissued any person who had a drug conviction their teaching license. Although at my fourth appearance before the board, the Practicing

Commission voted 5 to 4 to deny me…a glimmer of hope in a battle that appeared hopeless. I became a person who no longer had hope in the system…

In this life time, you are going to make mistakes…that's what happens… you make mistakes and learn from them…people make mistakes… most people need a second chance for some wrong they have committed…I not only paid for my mistake with the time I spent incarcerated but I paid the government $3,000.00 restitution taxes on money for distribution of illegal drugs, court costs, etc…I paid my debt to society and in return I was asking to be granted a second chance… to be allowed to do what every respectable man wants to do…take care of his family by earning a living. I wanted to provide for my family and at the same time help children from impoverished communities like mine see a way to participate as citizens in our country without having to make the mistakes that I made. I wanted to be involved in the educational system to help create positive change in their lives.

If it weren't for my son Joseph then I believe that I would have quit seeking my license after they denied me the first time…but I didn't want to teach my son to be a quitter…so I persevered…despite not hearing from God and possibly being out of His will for my life…I persevered…but this time it wasn't for me…it was for my son Joseph Demure Vick….I loved him that much…

Joseph would be the reason for me to fight even though I wanted so badly to quit this pursuit of my license year after year. I wanted to do something different with my life, that wouldn't ask of me to put my faith on the line…I wanted the easier road traveled. I couldn't, because every time that I look at my son Joseph I saw all my strengths…none of my weaknesses… I saw all my accomplishments…none of my failures… I saw in my son Joseph Demure Vick all that was pure and admirable inside Terrance Demure Vick. To my son…I wasn't a failure or a convicted drug dealer…I was his hero, and like all heroes…I got knocked down…but I always got up.

Because of this love for my son, I want to reflect on a letter that I wrote while in the delivery room awaiting for his birth…a day that I will never forget: February 23, 2005.

I share this letter that I wrote to my son with you because I don't understand how any man could abandon his children.

It is precisely because of this abandonment by fathers, in my opinion, that presently many urban youth, especially boys are dying... going to jail, and dropping out of school at a higher rate... than has ever been seen in our country's history.

I share this letter with you because I believe that as men, we have a God given responsibility to go home and save our children from self destruction.

Lastly, I share this letter with you because like many of you, I too, lacked certain parental tools that some receive from their parents...these tools could have possibly kept me choosing the wrong path ...but it was my choice.

I love my parents and I believe that they did the best that they could for me...but I believe that each generation is required to do better...this letter was the beginning for me.

February 23, 2005

Dear Joseph Demure Vick,

I'm writing this letter to let you know just how proud as a father I am of you. I couldn't hold back the tears, joy and anticipation of your arrival in this world. The greatest gift outside of my salvation and my marriage to your mother is your birth. Words cannot begin to express what I feel inside of me because of you, son. However, I will attempt to write my feelings so that you will always have a reference to how much I am committed to you and how much I love you, Joseph Demure Vick.

I don't really know where to start but I believe that I will begin by telling you that I love you with every fiber that is in me. My love for you surpasses all comprehension and understanding. God has blessed me with an opportunity to impart love, understanding, compassion and wisdom to you. I believe that the most important purpose in my life is to point you in the right direction, while providing wise counsel when you are faced with trials and tribulations. Believe me son, there will be trials and tribulations in your life but I will be there to help when you fall, and dust you off and place you back on track. I believe, my son, my responsibility is also to demonstrate before you how to walk a Godly life; to be a man that stands upright before God, society and his family; to be a man of honesty, integrity and character. A man that is not perfect but is also not prideful. A man that can admit when he is wrong and has made a mistake. I want to be a Father who has the courage to not quit in life but is willing to continue doing the things of God. I want to be a Father who continually expresses pride in his son's many accomplishments but also a Father who provides discipline when it is warranted.

I want to demonstrate before you son, how to properly treat women with respect, kindness and love. I pray that I model my best through my relationship with your mother, because there's no greater joy than to have a wife who completes you. A good wife is something to cherish. She will encourage you in ways that your Mother and I cannot.

Finally, my son I want to speak to your purpose. God has given you a name that speaks to the contributions that you will make to this society. A new legacy begins with you because you shall live in the land flowing with milk and honey, the promised land. Men shall seek advice, wealth and wisdom from you. You shall be the lender and not the borrower. You shall be above and not beneath. Where I struggled for years in my life, you will have victory. There will be no more famine because of you, Joseph.

To much that is given, remember much is required. I will always be there for you, even when I cross into the land of the non-living. I will never leave you Joseph, my beloved son.

Your Daddy
Terrance Demure Vick

Although I loved my son…these next four years nothing…and I mean nothing appears to be going good for me in my life…except being a father
I tried several different avenues to make more money…because of my inability to obtain my teaching license, I was so underpaid…so I tried

investing…no success…I tried promoting concerts, Rap and R&B…still no success.

Inside me, there was this empty feeling of being out of touch with God's will for my life…and although it didn't appear that God still had His hand on my life… I could still hear His voice calling me…

Lazarus…Honor your wife that your prayers may not be hindered.

Twelve
U-Tube Sensation

"Count it all joy when you fall into various trails, knowing that the testing of your faith produces patience. But let patience have its perfect work, that you may be perfect and complete, lacking nothing."
—James 1:2-4

Even though the Kansas Practicing Commission would not reissue me my teaching license, I still taught math at a middle school charter school in Kansas City, Missouri...Urban Community Leadership Academy.

I really enjoyed teaching at UCLA charter school...I loved the kids with whom I had contact. I felt that I was making a difference in their life, and that is what truly matters to me.

When you teach in an urban or inner city school, you have to make sure to teach the whole child. Your students have to know that you care about what they face everyday in their life...or it will become impossible to reach them.

I know that teaching as a career wasn't designed in her purest form to take the place of the family...but today's students require just that...for the teacher needs to be the parent, friend, counselor and policeman. They need compassion, direction, understanding, discipline and safety…all from the teacher because in most of their lives…the teacher is the only one to give them these essential elements of survival.

In my opinion, we are failing our urban and inner city youth…not because the students can't read and write or are two and three grade levels behind academically…no, no, no… it's because what these urban and inner city students need…are teachers…yes teachers, who can address the whole child, not just teach subject material..…I know its not fair to require the teacher to perform all of these duties but it's the job that is necessary…you will always see a huge teacher turnover rate in urban and inner city schools…the teachers become burned-out and just can't take it any more…it becomes too heavy of a burden.

However…I love the challenge of teaching students who are forced to achieve in spite of many obstacles. I enjoyed showing these students that they are more than just the dead situations from which many of them come…that they are all like **Lazarus…who have the ability to rise out of dead situations…they just need a champions…teachers who care.**

To say that I hadn't experience any success within my career would be grave error …my success came through teaching……I had started a freshman football team, that went 5-3 in its first year of existence, I took a 8th grade math class during the 2006-07 school year and 70% of my students met the Annual Yearly Progress (AYP) goal and I started an interest group boys, a Jr. Fraternity.

Those twelve boys in the Jr. Fraternity caused the nation to take notice of what I was doing at Urban Community Leadership Academy Charter School. Prior to this controversy…I can safely say…that no one outside of Kansas City, Missouri took any interest in what the students were being taught at Urban Community Leadership Academy…but because of the Jr. Fraternity u-tube controversy…everyone became concerned whether the students were being adequately taught…and I stood smack dead in the middle of it.

It all started in the 2007-2008 school year. In an attempt to change the culture of the building our principal required the entire teaching staff to start crew/interest groups for the students.

Unlike the other teachers, who were given the opportunity to choose which crew/interest group that they wanted to start …I was instructed to start a Fraternity group. She knew that I was in a fraternity and because of the popular interest in the recent movie "Stomp The Yard", she informed me that I would have a fraternity crew/interest group.

The first task for me was to develop a curriculum to engage the young men. Because this wasn't an actual fraternity…I was somewhat limited in what I could share with these boys…However, there were things from my fraternity which I thought would be vital to help these boys become responsible young men and create a bond among them. I taught the boys my fraternity's cardinal principles…Manhood, Scholarship, Perseverance and Uplift…public information if you search. I also taught the boys poems that they had to memorize…"Mother to Son", "Invictius", "Don't Quit" and "See It Through". I even gave the boys a name to call their fraternity line…Omega Alpha…which meant "The last shall be first."

I can truly say that these twelve boys not only improved their academics but they took an active leadership role in the school.

Because the group met in the morning for 45 minutes…we would meet in the basement of the school where I actually had the boys get in a line to give them a real experience of how pledging in a fraternity would be…each morning, many students in the building would come to the basement to see what these twelve boys were doing. They quickly became the envy of the school.

During this time, Barack Obama was campaigning to become the first African-American President of the United States.

The boys began asking me questions about Barack Obama. It was still early in the primary but once Barack Obama had won Iowa, everyone started to take notice…I know that I did. The boys and I would discuss topics like…can he win?…will someone shoot him dead if he does win?…and did I think that I would live to see an African-American man become President of the United States of America?…and my favorite…if Barack Obama could become president does that mean that they would have the same opportunity to become President of the United States of America?

Many questions…not many answers for them…but I told those twelve boys that they could become whatever they chose to become…it's your choice and it starts with what you do today…I truly believed that in my heart…but my heart was also telling me that Barack Obama, wasn't going to win…white folks wouldn't allow it…I believed that they could achieve anything but President of the United States…sad, I know…a slave mentality…and more importantly, I didn't have enough faith that my boys could one day achieve that goal.

Either way, Barack Obama was doing well and better than any one expected…and he was actually winning primaries…but it was his speech, "Race in America" that would give birth to the idea of an opportunity for the boys to perform.

I listened to this speech again and again. Some of the things that he was saying in the speech were exactly what the boys needed to hear. He was talking about accountability not only for students but for parents in the African-American community…I liked that.

I took excerpts from this speech and designed a chant that was entitled "Yes We Can." The boys created the movements. I required two things from them in order to perform this stomp…to say that because of Obama I'm inspired to become the next ????…they couldn't mention an athlete or entertainer…respectable careers, but I wanted these young men to begin to think about the possibility of a variety of achievable professions other than those two careers…secondly, the boys had to learn about a portion of his health care plan to present…since he and Hillary seem to make this a major issue while on the campaign…I wanted to see what his health care plan actually was.

The twelve boys learned and memorized that information in one week…you need to remember I only met with these boys for 45 minutes every morning…they learned this information at home… those of us who teach in an urban or inner city school know how challenging it is for our students to take home work and return it…but these boys were so into this performance that they learned it.

I first discussed this performance with my principal, and she thought this was the greatest thing since sliced bread…twelve boys in a single line reciting "Yes We Can" and being inspired by Barack Obama to attend college and make something of themselves...she loved it so much that she asked if the boys could perform it for the entire student body.

We performed this routine not once but twice, not just for the student body but parents, and our local Congresswoman...who had never been to this school before this performance, and also, the United States National Guard...who donated the boots and army pants that the boys wore while performing...big thanks, once again.

Everyone loved it and I was proud of what the boys had accomplished...I decided to place it on u-tube so the world could see what I see in our urban and inner city youth.

I informed the principal of my intentions and she said to first consult with an attorney and make sure that I had parental permission. I thought that if the performance was appropriate to perform in school then it would be appropriate to show the world. After I received the parents' permission, I placed it on u-tube in May of 2008...Barack Obama hadn't even won the Democrat Nomination. Because it was the end of the school year...no one paid attention to it...although all that would change in October of 2008...five months later.

While attending a math conference in Oklahoma City with our math department, I received a call on Saturday night, October 4, 2008 from our computer teacher who had recorded the video. He asked me to check the Utube site because some Neo-Nazi group had copied the video and placed it on their site to comment about the boys.

This Neo-Nazi group had mentioned that if Barack Obama was elected President, that this would be what our country could expect from our inner cities...an uprising from black youth. They would continue to say that this was the same way that Hitler had started his uprising by militarizing the youth...and because these boys were in army fatigues like my fraternity chapter wore...he was starting his own inner city youth militia.

Everyone was copying from this web site and making similar comments about the boys and how we have to keep Barack Obama from being elected President.

Wow...and Wow backwards...I couldn't believe that someone could draw this conclusion from the video when the boys were only saying how inspired they were to make something of themselves…the army fatigues were symbolic of my fraternity…that's it, nothing more. To give you an idea of how crazy this had become…from the time our computer teacher called me Saturday to my return to the classroom Monday morning…the video went from 37 hits to 450,000 hits in one day.

Monday, when I returned to my classroom, the school had already had calls from news stations across America wanting to know about this video that now had one million hits on Utube.

I thought to myself…if I had received a dollar from every hit…I would have become a millionaire over night.

The assistant principal called me to his office to ask me to remove the video from the internet so no one could view it anymore because the school was receiving more calls from the media than it could handle concerning this video as well as receiving a bomb threat. I informed him that I would remove it; however, there was no way to keep people from copying the video to their web sites.

The assistant principal asked me to go home on supervised suspension until the school could get a handle on this video controversy. I remember telling the assistant principal to be calm and to spin whatever negative press the school was receiving to positive press…I did nothing wrong, so why act as if I was guilty of something about which the school was knowledgeable.

I couldn't believe it…within one hour of me leaving the school all the local news media were informed that I had been suspended… what the …I hadn't even been told I was suspended from my principal and the media was already reporting it…and why was I being suspended…I placed this video on Utube last school year in May…and the school was made aware of my intentions to place it on Utube…what the…this is crazy! Lord…I did nothing wrong.

While I set at home suspended with pay, for the next three months…I became the topic of many television shows like The View, Fox News, CNN, MSNBC, BET, Dateline and nearly every national radio show in America…the discussion was always the same…should the teacher have been suspended?…did the teacher cross the line and push his/her political views upon the students?…who is this suspended teacher?

Lord...it's me again. I did nothing wrong...why is this happening to me Lord...why me, Lord? Why am I being persecuted again in the media Lord, for something good that I did...I can accept the first time, because I had broken the law...I understand that...but this time Lord...I did nothing wrong.

Lazarus..."Do not be afraid or dismayed because of this multitude, for the battle is not yours, but God's" 2nd Chronicles 20:15

My suspension continued until January 2009 at which time I was terminated...but I continued taking classes at Park University to complete my masters degree in Educational Administration. I no longer had a job teaching...but all my needs were being supplied by God.....and most importantly...I had peace through all this chaotic mess by which I was surrounded.

Thirteen

Never Would Have Made It...Without You!

"So shall My word be, that goes forth from my mouth; It shall not return to Me void, But it shall accomplish what I please, and it shall prosper in the thing for which I sent it."

—Isaiah 55:11

"Why do we go to school?"...I asked my son Joseph as I drive him to school.

"To learn Daddy."...he replies to me.

"Is there anything that you cannot learn?"...I asked.

"No Daddy."...is his answer.

"What are our principles?"

He replies, "Honesty, Integrity and Character."

This would be daily routine for the next nine months after my termination from Urban Community Leadership Academy Charter School. I can report that I'm not bitter or angry since my departure...as a matter of fact...I have peace and comfort knowing that all my financial needs will be provided. God has been faithful thus far in my life...why wouldn't He continue to be faithful to me.

In the past nine months there have been many positive changes to my life. The first and most important of these changes is that I remarried my wife and brought my family together.

You see it was God who continued to remind me to **honor your wife ...so that your prayers will not be hindered.** That's just what I did...I honored her and we were remarried on January 31, 2009. Nothing brings greater joy to a man than to have the opportunity to wake up every morning with his family in the same house. To honor God, we join hands every morning before we leave the house and pray together as a family that God will continue to keep us together and strengthen our union.

It's very moving to me to watch our son Joseph, pray to God, and thank God. Tears come to my eyes to think...how selfish I was! I never thought about how it affected my son that both his mother and I lived in separate homes. I always thought that because we both loved him and showered him with love that it didn't matter that we lived apart because he was too young to know the difference. He did recognize the difference... and I can report today that my son appears to be whole, the way all children should be, and he's truly happy. He has that security in knowing that Daddy's here and not going anywhere. If for some reason at night those bad monsters come into his room then he can call his Daddy who is in the next room.

These past nine months afforded me the opportunity to finish my masters degree from Park University. It amazes me that I was able to pay for my masters, while unemployed...it was all by the grace of God. Reminds me of what Bishop T.D. Jakes always says, "Favor Ain't Fair".

However, the greatest testimony to my faith would occur September 14, 2009. That was the date scheduled to meet before the Kansas Professional Practices Commission on my application for reissuing of my Kansas Professional Educator's License, something that I had failed to accomplish the previous four years. Although this time, circumstances appeared different because for the first time since I applied for my teaching license the Practices Commission had rescheduled my appointment from June 1, 2009 to September 14, 2009.

I viewed this change as if God removed certain people from the previous board, which had denied me the past four years, and appointed new people who would hear my story with an open mind and heart.

When your back is against the wall, you will look for any sign that gives you hope that just maybe what you have been wishing for is possible...and I was desperate for a gesture from God.

Something else that was different was the reuniting of my high school counselor/administrator with whom I hadn't spoken in over ten years. She was the only woman in my life other than my mother and wife, who demanded nothing but the very best from me.

With her, not attending college wasn't even an option…she put her money where her mouth was and paid for me to take the SAT and ACT when I was in high school. She was, however, very disappointed that I attended Garden City Community College instead of the University of Oklahoma. She was proud all the same that I did go to college.

She helped me receive the Grow Your Own Teacher scholarship that paid for my schooling at Wichita State University.

She demanded to attend the meeting for the fifth appearance before the Licensure Board on September 14, 2009.

To be totally honest…I didn't want her to drive to Topeka on my behalf and have to set through another meeting/trial. I can still remember her face and the disappointment she felt while she sat in the courtroom and listened to the District Attorney read the charges pending against me. The same charges on which I would later be convicted…No… it's safe to say that I didn't want her in that boardroom…I didn't want to disappoint her anymore.

I've come to discover, that the funny thing about love …is that you can't stop an individual from loving you unconditionally, regardless of what you do or say…and because of her involvement in my life over twenty years, she felt she had a right to come support me…and so that was final, she was coming to Topeka.

Lastly, my son and wife were going to go with me for the first time. As a family, we had been praying every morning for some closure to this teaching license issue and had decided that this would be my last attempt to get my license renewed in Kansas.

It would be my wife's words during our prayer time that would inspire the title of this book, **Your Mistake Is Not Your Signature**. Those simple, but yet powerful, six words would be the words that would give me the comfort of knowing that I couldn't and wouldn't carry this mistake any further than what I had already carried it. I was fully convinced in my heart that it was finally time for me to let it go.

I had believed God over ten years ago when He had spoken to me while I was still in prison that I would teach again. In the last five years, I had stopped depending on God and started relying upon my own ability and intellect to acquire my teaching license, only to discover that the Practices Commission wasn't impressed with my intellect or abilities, and so they continued to deny me time and time again.

Those six words, **Your Mistake Is Not Your Signature** gave me the assurance that if the Practices Commission did grant me my license it would be through God's grace and mercy and not of my doing.

My family and I were standing firm on the conviction that I would never travel down this road to Topeka, Kansas again.

September 14, 2009 finally arrived. I recall awaking earlier than my wife and son and going into our living room and falling on my knees and speaking with God. I wish I could report that I heard God's voice speaking to me…but I can't. I cried and cried some more pleading with God that I can no longer sign my name to this mistake.

I can't carry this burden…it had become too overwhelming…and I just can't do it anymore…still, no response from God.

Maybe God had forgotten his promise to me…I remember thinking while on my knees that I wasn't worthy of His promise …since I had been unfaithful to His word.

Either way, I told God with some boldness…**this is it…I refuse to put my family through this anymore…they deserve better from me.**

We dressed, ate breakfast and drove west on I-71 from Kansas City to Topeka, Kansas. No one said anything, except Joseph who asked where we were going and, are we there yet?

At some point on this hour-long trip, I looked at my wife and I wanted so badly to express to her…I'm sorry. Sorry for putting our family in this situation…sorry if I don't receive the verdict for which we have prayed.…sorry that I'm not providing the way a man should provide for his family…sorry that she has to work twelve hour long shifts as a nurse and go to school…sorry that I was unfaithful during our first marriage…but I didn't…I didn't say a word…but I wanted to tell her.!

She, on the other hand, must have sense that I was afraid… afraid of being disappointed…afraid that my son would see his father disappointed and she said to me, the only words spoken to each other on that journey…**Your Mistake Is No longer Your Signature…we will get through this together as a family.**

I looked away from my wife…it was the only way to keep me from crying.

We met my former counselor/administrator in the lobby of the board room and I introduce my family to her. She had changed…she no longer stood erect, a woman of distinguished pride, but she now walked with the assistance of a walker due to a hip injury that she had suffered…she still nevertheless, commanded respect and deference of all who encountered her.

She and my family were seated to the left of me as I took my place in a center chair in front of these nine board members, who would determine whether or not I was fit to have my Kansas teaching license reissued.

Again I noticed that there were no people of color on the board and some of the faces were familiar to me from past hearings…I quickly thought in my mind that God didn't change this board one bit…so this may not go well for me.

My counselor/administrator, barely able to stand, spoke first…to be honest I couldn't remember anything that she said except…If society is willing to give Michael Vick a second chance…then she hoped that the board would see fit to give me a second chance because I would touch the lives of many more children in a very significant way as an educator.

The board had no questions for her.

I stood for the first time and began to address the board…wish I could recall what I said, but if I put anything in writing I may be exaggerating the truth because the only thing that I remember is that…I cried…and cried some more.

I cried because my counselor/administrator, in her condition, had driven all the way to Topeka on my behalf because she loved me that much.

I cried because my son was there and in my mind I appeared to be inadequate…and I didn't want my son to see me helpless.

I cried because as I looked to my left…my wife was crying.

Everything was a blur to me…the only thing I remember saying to the board was…I refuse to any longer sign my name to this mistake. My action over ten years ago, has not only cost me everything but it is now costing my family dearly…I can't do this anymore…this is the last time I will ever come before this board…I lost my way by placing my faith in the decision of this board, instead of trusting God who has continued to provide for me and my family.

The board asked me questions about the U-tube situation…why did I make the decision to sell drugs in the first place…do I believe that teachers should be held to a higher standard and …they ask if they could review the copies of the book (three rough draft copies) which I brought with me incase they had any questions about what I had been doing since the last time I appeared before them.

I answered all the questions and departed the boardroom with my family, as I had always done, to wait for their verdict. While waiting outside the boardroom, I can tell you that I had peace…didn't matter what their decision was…I had peace in knowing that I really let it go and I no longer would sign my name to that awful mistake anymore. My counselor/administrator asked me what was I going to do if they reissued me my teaching license?

I told her…I didn't know, because I didn't want to appear confident, only to be disappointed again…but if they did grant me my license that would place me in a position to then receive my Missouri teaching license and my Administrative license as well….but I really didn't know what I would do. I knew that I wanted to help prevent other children from having the experiences I had as a result of my poor choices.

One of the gentlemen on the board came and instructed me that the Practices Commission had reached its decision and were awaiting me.

I told everyone to stay there because I was going into the boardroom alone…they understood.

I walked into the boardroom and the chairman read the verdict of the Practices Commission. The chairman said that the Kansas Practices Commission on this day, September 14, 2009 votes to **REISSUE MY KANSAS TEACHING LICENSE**…all those in favor say I…all those oppose say no…**THE VOTE WAS 6-2!**

I dropped my head and stood motionless and began to cry...several of the board members came and said to me congratulations and that they couldn't wait to read the book once it is published.

One of the women on the board approached and hugged me. She told me that she believes that I will do great things through my book, that it will touch many lives and prevent people from making similar mistakes...she said, "just keep going with God!"

I walked as best as I could and tried to share the information with those waiting for me...let's just say that... that was the longest embrace of my lifetime.

God had done it...and I wasn't even worthy of Him blessing me...but He remained true and faithful to the promise He had made to me over ten years ago while I sat in that prison.

This was the first time the practices commission had recommended to the State Board of Education to reissue a teacher license to anyone who had a drug conviction...GOD IS SOOO GOOD!

People ask me why I wrote this book...I wrote it to say to anyone who is listening, that even in this tough economy God is still in the business of blessing people who have the faith to believe that He is God...the stock market may crash, the automobile industry can go bankrupt, companies can close their doors, and people can lose their jobs...but He is still God and will provide for you if you have faith.

God inspired me to write about my life, reliving shameful and hurtful memories of mistakes that I had made time and time again. What I realized as I began to write...was that worrying about my job situation ceased to be a factor. I stopped wondering whether or not I will get an administrative position for the next school year...I even stopped wondering if Kansas would reissue my teaching license...and I learned to trust God and what He was doing in my life at this moment.

This book allowed me to reflect and understand that God has provided for me every time and in every situation...maybe not the way that I would have wanted...but He was there in every situation...even when I wasn't living according to His word...He was there.

When I was accepted into college... He was there. Facing the judge before sentencing... He was there. Making it through prison... He was there. Trying to find a job after returning home from prison... He was there. Trying to find a teaching job after having my license revoked... He was there. Restoring my marriage... He was there. Facing this U-tube controversy... He was there. Having my teaching license reissued...He was there. Writing this book...He was there. Every time it appeared that I was facing unbelievable odds...GOD was there.

Marvin Sapp's song "Never Could Have Made It" is playing on the radio as I'm driving Joseph to school...and my son looks at me and asks..."Daddy why are you crying?"

This is the first time I've heard this song since I started writing this book...I've heard this song a million times...but never in the three weeks since I began writing this book.

I assured Joseph that nothing was wrong...that Daddy is crying because he made it...and so will he.

Epilogue

On November 10 2009, the Kansas State Board of Education voted 7-2 not to accept the recommendation of the Professional Practices Commission to reissue my teaching license. What I will do now is unknown. The law states that a person is eligible to reapply for a teachers license after five years removed from the conviction if that person presents evidence that demonstrates the nature and seriousness of the conduct that resulted in the revocation of his/her license is no longer a factor in his/her fitness to engage in the profession of teaching and school administration. The Practices Commission voted 6-2, not a simple majority, but by 75% that it accepted that this evidence had been demonstrated. The question then becomes, what more can be done to see that the person is reissued a license? If having a drug conviction is so serious as to not merit this consideration, why isn't it stated in the law. Why have a person continue to seek justice when none is available.